The Dynamics GP
Power User Guidebook

with

Microsoft Dynamics GP
Versions 10.0 / 2010

by
Richard L. Whaley
Senior Business Consultant
and Microsoft MVP 2006-2008

Published by:

Accolade Publications, Inc.
Documentation for Software Users

Altamonte Springs, Florida
www.AccoladePublications.com

The MS Dynamics GP Series
The MS Dynamics GP Power User Guidebook

(c) 2010 Richard L. Whaley
World rights reserved.

Some images are the property of
Microsoft and are published with
permission.

Published by:
Accolade Publications, Inc.
Altamonte Springs, Florida USA 32714

Library of Congress Card Number: pending

ISBN: 1-931479-07-0

Manufactured in the United States of America

Introduction

Welcome aboard!

Whether your firm is just now implementing MS Dynamics GP, you are a new hire into a company that already utilizes the application, or you have been using MS Dynamics GP for a while and want to know more, this book is written especially for you.

MS Dynamics GP is a collection of a large number of modules that handle the information of business enterprises. The modules selected determine whether the software performs simple accounting, complex distribution, manufacturing, project management, retail operations, or a variety of other business specialties. But in all cases, navigating through the application is your primary challenge.

This book is designed to walk a user through MS Dynamics GP and provide an in-depth look at the user interface. Readers will learn everything from logging on and off the application through navigating to specific windows, using Smartlists, Custom Links, Business Alerts, configuring Lookups, and much more.

The individual applications, even down to General Ledger, Receivables Management, et cetera, are all covered in other books. The process of setting up the application is covered elsewhere. This book assumes:

1. MS Dynamics GP is installed at your firm and ready to run.

2. MS Dynamics GP is installed on your workstation and ready to run.

3. You have been assigned a user ID and password.

4. Your roles and rights have been assigned.

5. Your firm is using MS Dynamics GP Version 10 or newer.

With this in mind, let's look at MS Dynamics GP!

Richard L. Whaley
Author, Senior Consultant

Dynamics GP for New Users

I. Logging In to MS Dynamics GP

Launching MS Dynamics GP varies greatly and depends on how the firm has installed the application on the desktop. Some users need to browse the Start Menu, find Microsoft Dynamics →GP and select the application. Others will find different names and paths in use or an icon on the desktop.

As the application launches, the Welcome to Microsoft Dynamics GP window will display. This is the initial logon window for the application.

The **Server** field contains (or should contain) the name of the ODBC connection to the SQL server holding the MS Dynamics GP databases. The team that implemented the firm's software should know and provide the server name. Once set, this field will not change unless someone changes it purposefully. Accept the default entry.

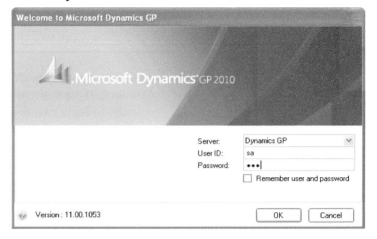

Enter the assigned **User ID** and **Password** and click OK to begin the login process.

Users running Version 2010 or newer will notice an additional field. The Welcome to MS Dynamics window has a "remember me" check box. If the System Manager has enabled this functionality, users can mark the Remember User and Password and automatically login when MS Dynamics GP is launched.

By clicking the Remember User and Password box, the system will remember the user logging into MS Dynamics GP on the current workstation and that user's password. The next time the user launches MS Dynamics GP, they will be automatically logged in.

Note that the current version of the application is displayed in the lower left corner of this window. All users on an installation of MS Dynamics GP must be using the same version. Also, the workstation hosting the client application must be logged into the network before MS Dynamics GP is started or access to the database will be denied.

Company Login

Microsoft Dynamics·GP 2010

Company:	Accolade Publications, Inc.
	☐ Remember this company
Server	Dynamics GP
User ID	sa
Current Users	1
Users Allowed	4095

[Change User...]   [OK]   [Cancel]

The Company Login window will display. This window allows the user to select a company. If the firm operates more than one company on this installation of MS Dynamics GP, each company may have a different database and set of records. Click the pull down list arrow to show a list of valid companies. If only one company is supported or the user is only allowed into one company, this list will only show that one company. MS Dynamics GP security can limit users to specific companies and prevent their access to other companies.

The other information on this window is for information only. The Server and User ID entered on the first screen is repeated for validation. The count of Current Users that are already logged in are shown along with the maximum number of Users Allowed. If the Current User count is equal to the Users Allowed, any attempt to login past this point will be blocked. Contact the System Administrator and ask that some users be asked to log out. If this situation repeats itself frequently, the firm may need to license additional users.

The Change User button on this window will take the user back to the initial login window. There, a different user ID and password can be entered.

Click OK to complete the login process. The Home Page for the user should be displayed.

Users running Versions 2010 or newer will notice an additional field. The Company Login window has a "remember me" check box as well. If the System Manager has enabled this functionality, users can mark the Remember This Company check box on the Company Login window. If a firm has multiple companies and the user has access to multiple companies, selecting a company and checking the Remember this Company check box will cause the system to default to the selected company when MS Dynamics GP is launched the next time.

In order for this functionality to work, the System Manager must check the Enable Remember User check box in the System Preferences window (see Section XIII.F. for information on completing the System Preferences window).

First Login

If this is the first time that a new user ID has been used to log into MS Dynamics GP, the system will display a Welcome to Microsoft Dynamics GP message and the Select Home Page window.

Please see Chapter XII.C.2. for information on completing this window.

II. Logging Out of MS Dynamics GP

Process Monitor

A special function in MS Dynamics GP displays any processes running in the background. This is called the Process Monitor.

Generally, the Process Monitor can be found under Microsoft Dynamics GP. If the application will not close and says there are "Processes Running that Must Complete First", watch the Process Monitor to determine when all tasks are complete.

When a user has completed their work in MS Dynamics GP, it is important that they properly logout. When the user first logged in, a connection was established between the application software on the user's workstation and the server holding the firm's database. Until the user logs out, that connection is maintained.

Simply turning the workstation off at the end of the day is NOT sufficient or proper. Turning off the workstation shuts down the desktop but does not release the connection established with the server. The server will believe that the user is still working and keep resources reserved for the user. This can affect certain nightly processes and will keep at least one user account reserved, potentially keeping others from using MS Dynamics GP.

To properly log off, either:

Click on Microsoft Dynamics GP and pick Exit from the menu that is displayed, or

Click on the X in the upper right corner of the Microsoft Dynamics GP window.

Either of these will close the application and any other windows the application has opened. If transactions are in process, the user may be notified to complete transactions or save data prior to closing the application. Sometimes, processes will be executing that do not show on the desktop. It may be necessary to check the Process Monitor and wait until those processes are complete.

III. The MS Dynamics GP Desktop

MicroSoft has spent considerable effort to make the MS Dynamics GP product lines match the look-and-feel of the Office product line. Once logged in, the user is presented with a familiar looking desktop. The address bar seen in Internet Explorer runs across the top of the window, while the well know tool bar menus are prominent. A band of tool bar icons, customized to the user's needs is present.

Down the left side, the Navigation Pane is found. An explorer display in the top half of the Navigation Pane allows access to short cuts for the selected application. Tiles in the bottom half allow selection of the primary module for the user.

In the center of the window, the Content Pane shows a configured Home Page for the user. From this starting point, easy access to all of the MS Dynamics GP functions can be obtained.

Address Bar

Tool Bar

Content Pane showing Home Page

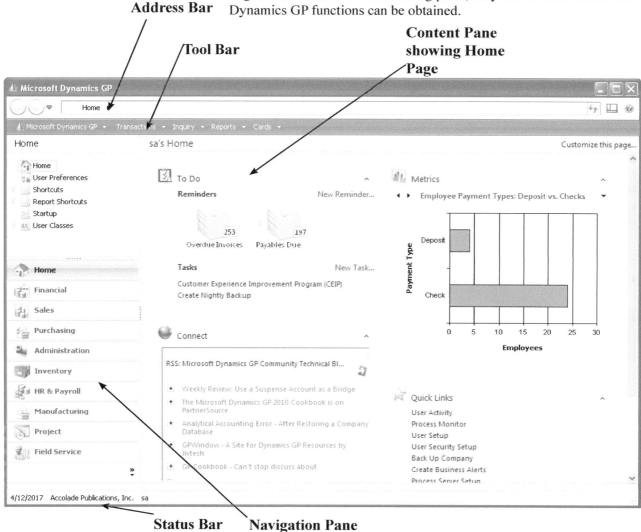

Status Bar   **Navigation Pane**

III.A.   The Address Bar

The top line of the desktop contains Navigation Buttons, the Address Bar, the Layout button, and the Help button.

Like Internet Explorer, the Address bar shows the current location within the application. As a user selects modules and tasks, the contents of the address bar will follow. Users can also use the Address bar to navigate through the application.

The Navigation buttons allow the user to easily return to previous selections. Use the Back button to move to the prior selection and the Next button to return to more recent selections. The Pull Down Arrow to the right of the Navigation buttons show a Most Recently Used sequence of selections. Clicking on one of the selections in this list will return the user to that selection.

The Layout Icon ( ), found to the right of the Address bar, allows the user to customize the general MS Dynamics GP desktop. This includes selecting Tool Bars to be displayed, turning the Navigation Pane on and off, and customizing these areas. Customization of the desktop is covered in Chapter XIII of this text.

The last icon on the Address Bar is the Help Icon ( ). This opens a Windows style help browser for the MS Dynamics GP application. The Help Icon can be found on almost every MS Dynamics GP window.

III.B.   The Tool Bar

The Tool Bar Menu allow users to open cards, transactions, inquiries, and other screens using cascading drop-down menus or shortcut icons. This classic menu system provides an easy transition to the MS Dynamics GP User Interface (UI). In the image below, the user has selected Transactions → Sales → Sales Transaction Entry, using the Tool Bar Menus causing the Sales Transaction Entry window to open.

Microsoft Dynamics GP uses an independent window design. Notice first that the Sales Transaction Entry task is in a separate window from the Microsoft Dynamics User Desktop. Each task window is found in a completely separate window with their own frame and menu bar. They float outside of the User Desktop and can be found on top of the Desktop window or beneath it!

An icon appears in the Windows task bar for every MS Dynamics GP window that is open. If ever a window is "lost", look for the icon and click it. Most likely, the lost window is simply hidden beneath another window.

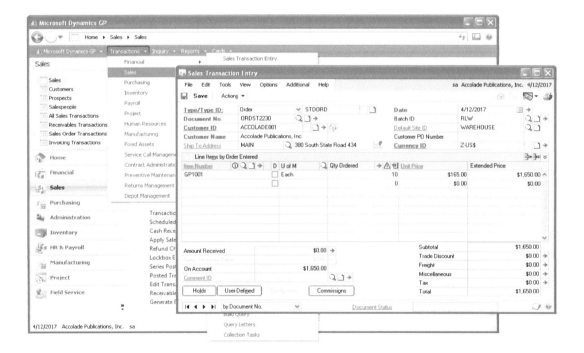

III.C. The Navigation Pane

The Navigation Pane runs down the left side of the MS Dynamics GP desktop and consists of two parts. The upper half contains an explorer tree containing folders and shortcuts to tasks and list pages. The lower half contains tiles representing the software series' licensed to the site. Selecting a tile in the lower half of the Navigation Pane changes both the content of the upper half of the pane as well as the options available in the Content Pane. In addition to the software series, two special tiles represent the Home Page and an Administration Page.

Note: If the Navigation Pane is not visible, click on the Layout button on the Address bar and check Navigation Pane.

Selecting a tile in the lower half of the Navigation Pane causes the upper half of the Navigation pane to display an explorer offering the pallets for the series on the first branch of the explorer as well as a series of Lists in the remaining branches. The first branch of the explorer displays the various menus and tasks for the series in the Content Pane.

The lower half of the Navigation Pane consists of tiles representing the various product series as well as a special Home and Administration tile. The amount of space occupied by the upper and lower halves of the Navigation Pane can be changed by moving the divider bar between the two sections.

The lowest tile is reserved for overflow icons. When the lower half of the Navigation Pane is too small to display all of the product series, small icons will be placed on the bottom tile, one for each of the overflow series.

An expansion arrow in the lowest tile opens a Configuration Menu.

Most of the configuration options for the Navigation Pane apply only to the Home Tile. These options allow users to add Windows, SmartLists, Macros, and External Tasks to the upper half of the Home Navigation Pane.

Users can add windows to Shortcuts in two manners. Either open the Add Window Shortcut window, drill down to the desired window, and click the Add button to place the selected window in the shortcuts list of the Home Navigation Explorer, or the user can open the desired window, click on the File menu in the new window, and click on the Add to Shortcuts option.

(The Home Navigation Explorer is the list of folders and shortcuts displayed in the top half of the Navigation Pane when the Home Tile is selected.)

Test or Training Company

Most installations of MS Dynamics GP have a training company. This allows users to try out new functions in a "sand-box" environment, where mistakes can be ignored.

Talk to the system administrator to find out if there is a training company available.

A Subtle Difference in Icons

The icons that appear in the Navigation Pane Explorer have minor differences with a major difference in meaning. Notice in the example below that there are actually 3 different icons shown.

The first icon (labeled Sales) represents a menu page. The second icon (labeled Customers) represents a primary List that cannot be modified by the user. The third icon (labeled Customers in....) represents a modified List or List Favorite with sorts and selects defined by the user.

The arrow in front of the Customers icon is the List Expansion Arrow. Pointed down as it is here shows the List Favorites under that Primary List. If it points directly toward the Primary List, it indicates that the Explorer branch is collapsed but that Favorites exist.

The Navigation Pane Options allow the user to modify the Tiles displayed. The Navigation Pane Options window can be opened by selecting it from the configuration menu or by right clicking on any series tile.

Each of the available tiles or buttons (a large button is normally called a tile, especially when they are displayed next to each other like the tiles on a wall or floor) can be turned on or off or moved in the list. The user can change the order in which the tiles are displayed in the Navigation Pane by highlighting a tile and clicking the Move Up or Move Down button. Tiles can be removed from the Navigation Pane display by removing the check box next to the button's name in the list in the Navigation Pane Options.

Selecting the Administration Tile displays the Administration Tasks in the Content Pane and the Administration Navigation Explorer. These menus contain the system tools and configuration options.

Other tiles select the tasks and Lists for the various series in the application. The majority of the branches on the various different Navigation Explorers are List.

Note: The security rights granted to a user by the system administrator may limit the tiles, menus, and options that can be seen. Do not panic if a tile is mentioned here that cannot be seen.

III.D.   The Status Bar

The Status Bar is displayed across the bottom of the MS Dynamics GP desktop. It shows the current system date, the company the user is logged into, and the User ID of the current user. All three of these items can be changed by simply clicking on them.

When the user clicks on the date, the User Date window opens. The date can be changed here and will affect all transactions entered from the time the date is changed forward.

Clicking on the company name opens the second login window and allows the user to close the current company and select a different company. This assumes that the current installation of MS Dynamics GP is supporting more than one company.

Clicking on the User ID in the status bar opens the first login window and allows the user to log back into the application with a different ID.

III.E.   *The Content Pane*

The Content Pane occupies the majority of the space on the MS Dynamics GP desktop. The information displayed in this area changes based on the Series Tile and Navigation Explorer option selected. Application menus, list panes, report lists, and more can be displayed in the Content Pane. Selecting the Home tile causes the user's Home Page to be displayed in the Content Pane. This is the default display when a user first logs in to MS Dynamics GP.

III.E.1.   The Home Page

The contents of the Home Page will vary from user to user and from site to site. MS Dynamics GP contains a list of Home Page configurations designed for specific types of users. The layout can also be tailored to the specific needs of the user. The general features of the Home Page will be discussed here. Configuring the Home Page is discussed in Chapter XIII.C. of this manual.

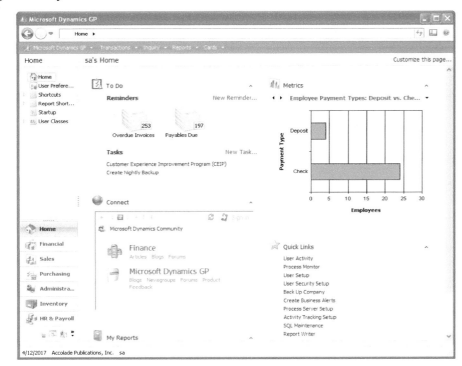

The Home Page Pane can contain up to 5 major sections: To Do's, Quick Links, Microsoft Outlook, Metrics, and My Reports.

The To-Do Section of the Home Pane is split into two sections: Reminders and Tasks

III.E.1.a.   Reminders

Reminders are those items displayed on the desktop that provide users with key performance indicators (KPI) related to their particular job and responsibilities within the firm. Reminders can be tailored per user and provide each MS Dynamics GP user with the information they need to better perform their job.

For example, the controller may want displays of the cash position of the firm while the receivables manager wants to know outstanding collectibles and past due customer totals. The shipping operations manager will find the number of open orders and the number of orders scheduled for shipment within the next 3 days helpful information. All of this and more can be displayed in the reminders.

There are two kinds of reminders, predefined and custom reminders. The predefined reminders are hard coded in the system and can be selected for display by checking a box. Custom reminders are tied to SmartLists. Adding or deleting reminders from the desktop is discussed in Chapter XIII.C.3.a.

In Versions 2010 and above, The Reminders section of the desktop, if displayed, can show each item as the standard list item with a count of items or it can be displayed as an icon scaled according to the quantity of items.

III.E.1.b.   Tasks

The task list is a listing of pre-scheduled tasks the user needs to perform. The task is added to the user's list and a date and frequency established. When the user performs the task, it will be removed from the task list until the next scheduled time.

For example, a monthly report may need to be printed at the first of each month. A task can be defined to remind the user to print this report. Once the report is printed, it will be removed from the task list until the next month when it needs to be printed again.

To perform a task, simply click on the task in the list. The appropriate window will be opened.

See Chapter XIII.C.3.b. for information on creating new tasks.

III.E.1.c.   Quick Links

Quick Links, like Reminder-Tasks are jobs that the user needs to perform. Rather than scheduled jobs, however, the most commonly performed tasks for the user are listed in the Quick Links. Simply clicking on the Quick Link opens the window necessary to perform the task.

Quick Links do not disappear from the Home Pane when they have been completed. They remain to be selected as frequently as necessary. For example, if a user is always working in the Sales Transaction Entry window, that window may be listed in the Quick Links. Rather than clicking on Transactions → Sales → Sales Transaction Entry, the user can simply click the Quick Link for Sales Transaction Entry.

Instructions for adding or removing Quick Links can be found in Chapter XIII.C.4. of this book.

III.E.1.d.   MicroSoft Outlook

If the firm uses MicroSoft Outlook, the user's outlook account can be linked to the MS Dynamics GP Home Pane. Clicking on this link will open Outlook.

III.E.1.e.   Metrics

Depending on the user desktop role, several graphs can be displayed. VCR style arrows next to the title of the chart allows the user to move from one chart to another. A pull-down arrow shows a list of charts. The charts are dynamically updated from data contained in the system.

In Version 10, the metrics displayed on the Home Page are selected from a predefined list of graphs and charts. In Version 2010, the user or a System Administrator can create additional metrics for display.

To enable the use of externally created metrics, open the Reporting Tools Setup window. At the bottom of this window is a pair of check boxes. Check the Enable SQL Server Reporting Services Home Page Metrics to enable new metrics to be generated using SRS. Check the "Charts and KPIs have been deployed to a Sharepoint Server" if the SRS reports are stored on the firm's Sharepoint server.

Make sure the remainder of this window is setup correctly. SQL Reporting Services must be properly deployed for this function to work. See Accolade's *Customizing GP with The Builders* for information on configuring these pages.

Once SQL Server Reporting Services Home Page Metrics are enabled, a message is displayed telling the user that the MS Office Web Components metrics (the default metrics) will not be available. If the default SRS reports have been properly deployed, these metrics should be duplicated in the list of SRS documents.

III.E.1.f.   My Reports

MS Dynamics GP contains a large number of reports. Each user has a handful of those reports that he or she runs frequently. These favorites can be added to the My Reports list and executed from the Home Pane. In Chapter VI. on printing reports, the process of adding reports to the Home Pane My Reports list is discussed.

To execute a report on the list, simply click the report.

Microsoft has continued to enhance the Reporting Lists in Version 2010. Now, in addition to a full Reports List, the system contains a separate list of MS Dynamics GP Reports (from the Report Writer and the Options configured through the standard application) and a separate list of SmartList Favorites.

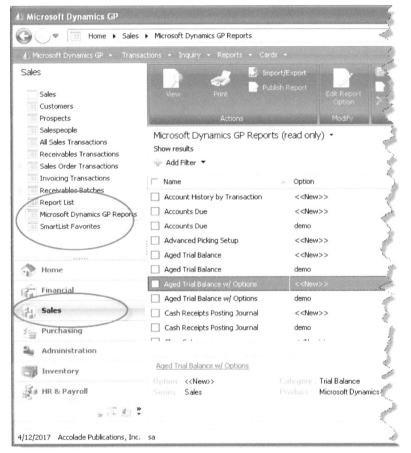

For MS Dynamics GP Reports, users no longer need to select Reports, Reports Group, then find a report by name. Instead, the user clicks on the series tile, then Microsoft Dynamics GP Reports, and a list of all of the base reports and configured options is listed. The user can scroll down the list or use a filter to locate the report.

If a user clicks on a report name that is marked <<New>> in the Option column, they can create and save a new option by entering the desired parameters.

See Chapter VI for detailed instructions on defining Report Options.

Users that want to launch SmartList Favorites, including the default * Favorite can display a list of Favorites by clicking on the appropriate leaf in the Navigation Pane. This opens a list of Favorites in the Content Pane.

If the user launches the SmartList listing from one of the Series' Navigation explorers, the Favorites for that Series are displayed. If the user launches the SmartList listing from the Home tile, all Favorites are listed.

As with MS Dynamics GP Reports, users can open a SmartList Favorite, make changes to the columns or selects, and save the new list as a new Favorite. The new Favorite will appear on the Content Pane list of Favorites when it is refreshed.

III.E.2.   List View Functions

The List Functions, available in the Lists Pane, provide a powerful way to access, modify, and report on the data contained within the MS Dynamics GP application. From a single screen, a list of records (customers, vendors, inventory items, employees, et cetera) can be displayed, filters applied to limit the list, the records selected for editing, new records added, reports printed, and selected functions performed.

But the real power of this feature is how these functions are managed.

When a business series (Financial, Sales, Purchasing, Inventory, et cetera) is selected in either the Address Bar or the Navigation Pane, the Content Pane displays a set of functions for the series and the Navigation Explorer offers branches with a variety of Lists. For example, if the Sales series is selected, Customers, Prospects, Salespeople, All Sales Transactions, Receivables Transactions, Sales Order Transactions, Invoicing Transactions, Receivables Batches, and Reports List options are displayed. Some of these selections (Sales Order Transactions and Receivables Batches in our example) are actually groups of options that can be expanded by clicking on the expansion arrow to the left of the option in the list, showing Views of the Primary List.

Clicking on one of the Lists in the Navigation Explorer pane changes the Contents Pane, presenting a List View with a four section display of functions specific to the option selected.

One section of the display, the **Filters Pane,** provides a place for the user to enter selection criteria. The restrictions entered here limit the list of customers, prospects, items, et cetera displayed. The second section, the **Action Pane,** provides a group of Actions that can be performed for the records displayed in the list. The third section is the actual **List Pane** displaying the selected records while the bottom section, the **Information Pane**, displays details of one of the selected records.

Filter Pane

Action Pane

List Pane

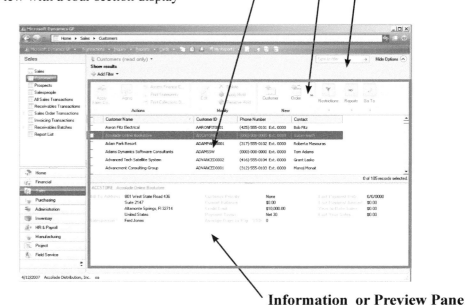

Information or Preview Pane

III.E.2.a.   The Action Pane

The Action Pane provides a series of functions that can be performed on the records displayed in the List Pane. The contents of the Action Pane will change from one list to another. When a user creates customized List Views (see below) the user can select which actions will be available for that view. The Actions offered should be the most frequently performed tasks for the List View being defined. This allows a user to customize their desktop and organize their most frequently performed tasks into a single desktop for each role.

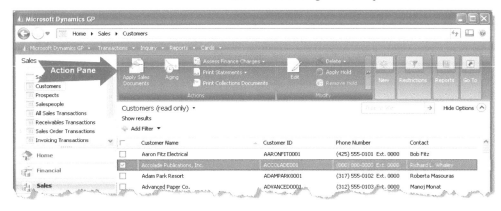

The Action Pane is organized into groups of functions. The Actions displayed can include record edit screens, new record creation, new transaction creation actions, reports, inquiries, Go To's, and export functions.

The Actions listed are performed on the records found in the List Pane. The valid Actions will change depending on the selections made in the List Pane. For example, if one record in the List Pane is selected, Edit Actions are valid. If multiple records are selected in the List Pane, the Edit Action is dimmed and will not function as this button typically opens a window that acts on a single record at a time. However, reports can be run that show only the multiple records selected. Holds can be placed on or removed from the multiple records selected with a single action. (Holds mean different things to different kinds of records. Consult the documentation for the specific module for information on the restrictions that holds place on various records.)

Take, for example, the Go To Actions for the Accounts in the Financial Series. These include View Transactions, Detail Inquiry, Summary Inquiry, and Send to Excel. If one account in the List Pane is checked, all of these Actions are active. Clicking on the View Transactions will open the Account Transactions List for the selected account. Clicking on the Detail Inquiry will open the Detail Inquiry window for the selected account. However, if more than one account is checked, only the Export to Excel option is active. Each of the accounts checked will appear in the resulting Excel spreadsheet. None of the other Go To Actions will be active as these actions only function for a single account.

The ability for an Action to work for more than one selected record in the List Pane provides some interesting abilities. Take, for example the Customer List in the Sales Series. One of the Actions is to Apply Holds to accounts. The filter functions can be used to reduce the list to selected customer accounts, then several specific customer records can be checked. When the Apply Hold Action is clicked, a hold will be automatically applied to each of the marked customers. A message is displayed showing the results of the action.

Numerous Actions work on multiple records like the Apply Hold Action. These include (among others) the printing of many reports, application of finance charges, deletion of records, and exporting of the selected records to Excel.

Selecting the Actions available is covered in Chapter XIII.D.3 of this book.

III.E.2.b.   Filters

In a live database system, Lists could be long! Consider, for example, a list of inventory transactions for a firm that moves hundreds of products daily and has been using MS Dynamics GP for several years. Fortunately, restrictions are provided and, until the user changes the restrictions, only transactions within the last 90 days are displayed. This restriction, however, is easily changed by clicking on the Restriction icon in the Action Pane and selecting a different restriction. A variety of standard date ranges and a custom date range is provided. Once a new restriction is selected, it will remain selected even after the application is closed until the user changes the restriction again.

The data in the list is presented in columns that are originally sequenced in an order specified by the person that created the list. The sequence of columns can however be changed by the user. Simply pick up a column title and move it to the desired position in the list.

The Lists are also sorted. The sort order is indicated by an up or down arrow to the left of the column title used to sequence the list. The user can change the sort by clicking on any column. The list will be sorted by that column. Clicking the same column again will change the sort order from ascending to descending.

MS Dynamics GP is delivered with a group of standard lists as well as a number of customized versions of these lists. Users can create their own customized lists from the existing lists. The process involves entering filters to specify a subset of the records displayed and then saving the specifications under a new name. These new lists are called List Views.

Select a list that contains the information desired. This list is then shortened to a more concise list by applying a series of filters. Filters can be logical using And, Or, Not, or Either statements. Fields are matched to user provided data and can be required to exactly match, begin with, contain, be greater than, less than, or not equal to the user data. Fields that are empty can also be selected.

Fairly complex conditional statements can be constructed using combinations of the comparison types and logical operators.

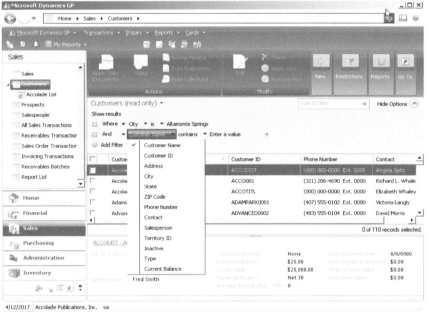

Each piece of the filter is added by clicking on the Add Filter prompt. The Logical Operator type is selected from a pull down list. The field to be used in the comparison is then selected from a pull down list. Next, the comparison type is selected and finally, the data to be used to limit the list is entered. Additional statements can be added by clicking on the Add Filter prompt until the logical statement is complete and the desired data is shown in the list.

Once the desired filter is built, it can be saved. The user clicks on the pull down arrow ( ) next to the title line of the original list. Select the Save As... option on the pull down menu and enter a name for the new list. The new list will be listed as a variation of the original list. It will be found in the Navigation Pane Explorer by expanding the primary list from which it was created. For example, if a customer list is modified to show only customers in a specified state and is saved, the new list option will be displayed in the Navigation Pane Explorer when the expansion arrow next to Customers is clicked.

If the user clicks Add to the Navigation Pane as a Shortcut, the name of the new list is added to the Home Navigation Explorer. It can be seen in the Navigation Explorer when the Home Tile is clicked and the Home Page displayed in the Content Pane. Clicking on the entry will open the new list in the Content Pane immediately.

If the user clicks Add to the Home Page, the name of the new list will be added to the Home Page itself and displayed in the Content Pane under Quick Links. The new list can then be displayed by clicking on the Quick Link.

To delete a List View, select the list from the Navigation Pane Explorer, click on the pull down arrow next to the list name in the Content Pane, and select Delete. A list can be renamed by selecting the list from the Navigation Pane Explorer, clicking on the pull down arrow next to the list name in the Content Pane, and selecting Rename.

III.E.2.c.   The List Pane

The List Pane contains a list of records from the topic list selected in the Navigation Explorer.

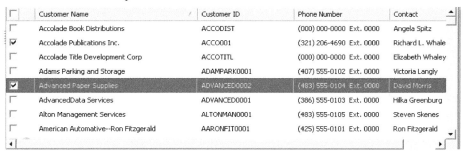

Data in the List Pane appears in columns. Each column can be moved left or right in the list by simply clicking on the column name and dragging it to the desired position.

The list is sorted by one of the columns. To change the sort, click on the desired column. Alternately clicking on the same column changes the sort from ascending to descending and back again.

A check box in the first column allows the user to select specific records. Various actions can be performed on the selected records. File maintenance functions can be performed on single records only, while some update processes and reports can be performed on multiple records at one time.

For example, if the Sales tile is selected in the Navigation Pane and the Customer List is selected in the Navigation Explorer, a list of customers will appear in the List Pane. Actions available include editing customer records, applying and removing holds, and accessing finance charges.

The edit function can only be performed on one customer at a time. Selecting one customer in the List Pane will activate this function while selecting more than one customer will inactivate the edit function.

Holds can be placed and removed from multiple records. Selecting one or more customers that are not on hold will cause the Apply Hold action to become active. Clicking the button will place the selected customers on hold.

Holds can only be removed from customers that are already on hold. Selecting one or more customers that are already on hold will cause the Remove Hold action to become active. Clicking that button will remove the hold from the selected customer or group of customers.

Finance charges can be assessed on groups of customers as well. Select the customers to access finance charges on and click this action. Finance charges will be calculated based on settings in the Customer Card and applied to the account (See *Understanding Receivables Management* from Accolade Publications, Inc. for more information on finance charges.)

Lists can be selected and favorites created. See Chapter XIII.D. for information on selecting lists and creating List Views.

Here is another great idea in an Ivory Tower that will be slow to be adopted if at all. Instant messaging between the firm and it's customers or vendors is now supported from within MS Dynamics GP in Versions 2010 and above. Once configured, users will be able to see the customers and/or vendors that are online and those customers and/or vendors will be able to see your users that are online. Messaging communications can be initiated immediately.

The problem is that most messaging systems, unlike the telephone systems, do not roll calls over to someone that is not already busy nor reply with a voice mail message. They just popup and wait for an immediate reply, even if the user is at lunch and still logged in or working with another customer.

For smaller firms, and with a bit more refinement, this idea is good. Right now it is too green in this author's opinion. However, here is how to implement and use this feature.

First, Microsoft Office Communicator must be installed. Discuss this requirement with the systems support team for the firm. Installation of the Microsoft Office Communicator is outside of the scope of this book.

Once Microsoft Office Communicator is installed and the application configured, the Navigation lists of vendors, customers, or employees will display a special icon. These icons will indicate that the marked person is online and available for an instant communication.

III.E.2.d. The Information Pane

The Information Pane provides a brief look as a selected record from
the List Pane. For example, if the Sales tile is
selected in the Navigation Pane and the Customer
List is selected in the Navigation Explorer, a list of
customers appears in the List Pane. Clicking on one
of those customers will cause the basic demograph-
ics for the customer (name, address, phone numbers, contact names, customer IDs, et cetera) to be
displayed in the Information Pane.

Double clicking on the hyper-link in the Information Pane will open the maintenance window for
the record, allowing the data to be edited. The user must have security
rights to the maintenance window or it will not be displayed.

III.E.3. The Menu View

Selecting the first item on the Navigation Explorer for any module
causes the Menu View to be displayed in the Contents Pane. This
provides a full set of menus on the desktop for all of
the functions allowed by security for the user.

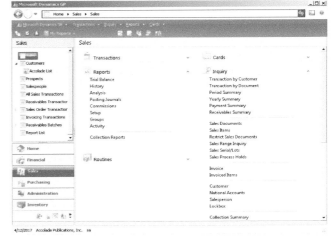

Tasks are grouped into an expandable explorer format of their own in the Menu View. Generally, tasks
will be grouped into Transactions, Cards, Reports,
Inquiries, Utilities, Routines, and Setup. Each of
these major groupings can be expanded (shown) or
collapsed (hidden) by clicking on the arrow to the
right of the group label.

When a group is expanded. some options will call
specific tasks while others will represent groups of
tasks. The groups of tasks will have a plus (+) or
minus (-) sign to the left of the option. Click on the
plus (+) sign to expand the option or the minus (-)
sign to collapse the option.

To execute any of the tasks on the menu, simply click on the option.
The appropriate Task Window will open. The general characteristics of
the Task Windows is described in Chapter IV of this book. The specific
functions of each task window are defined in the documentation on
each module of MS Dynamics GP.

III.E.4.   The Reports List View

The Reports List View is a special list view that displays the available reports for a module. When the appropriate module is selected in the Navigation Tiles and the Reports List from the Navigation Explorer, the list of available reports for the module will be displayed in the List Pane. The Action Pane will display tasks specific to the generation of the reports.

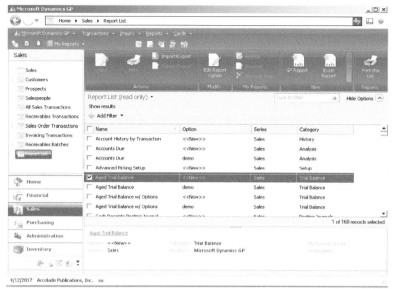

Each report has a set of options or parameters associated with it. Chapter VI.A. describes how the Report Options are defined and saved. However, when the report is printed, the options frequently need to be changed.

For example, the Customer List has options that include the first and last customer to appear on the report. An Ageing Report needs an effective date. These parameters are part of the information stored with the report.

To print a report, select it from the list displayed. (Check the box.) To change the parameters for the report, click on the Action button titled Edit Report Option. The Report Options window for the selected report will be displayed. The parameters can be modified as required and the report generated.

To see the My Reports list, select Administration. In the Administration Navigation Explorer, select Report List or My Reports.

Report lists can become very long. MS Dynamics GP is delivered with hundreds of standard reports. Users can add reports and pre-configured option sets for reports, resulting in an extensive series of reports on any list. The reports filters can be very helpful in locating any desired report in any report list.

In the Type To Filter, type a few characters or a phrase that appears in the desired report's name. Click the action arrow at the end of the field and the list of report will shorten to show only those reports containing the phrase. For more complex searches, filters similar to SmartList filters can be used.

IV. Task Windows

The business of the firm is performed in the Task Windows. Windows are provided with the application for the creation of master records (GL accounts, customers, vendors, inventory items, et cetera), the processing of transactions (sales order entry, purchasing, et cetera), viewing data through inquiries, the printing of reports, and other necessary support functions.

In the next few pages we will discuss the common features of Task Windows. This includes launching them, the common features of the windows, the several different types of windows, et cetera. What will not be discussed are the various tasks of each application. Separate documentation is available for sales processing, purchasing, receivables, payables, et cetera. Those texts discuss the applications, and the common characteristics of the windows.

IV.A.   Launching Task Windows

Task windows can be launched from a variety of locations. This includes the Navigation Pane, the Task Menus and Shortcuts, the Address Bar, et cetera. Task windows can even be launched from SmartLists and other Task Window.

In the next few paragraphs, at least 6 different ways to launch a task window are described. No user should have a problem getting to their desired application's task window.

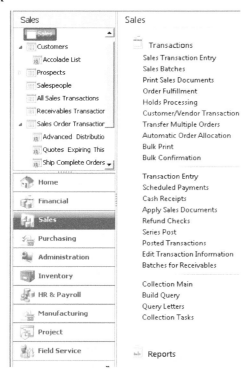

MS Dynamics GP Security settings apply to every option discussed below. If a user does not have the authority to open a specific task window, the application will not allow the window to be opened no matter how it is selected.

IV.A.1   From the Navigation Pane

As has been discussed in the earlier chapters of this book, task windows can be launched using the Navigation Pane. Select first a module or series such as Financial, Sales, Purchasing, et cetera by clicking on the tile in the lower section of the Navigation Pane. The module's Navigation Explorer will be displayed in the upper portion of the pane. By default, the Menu View for the selected module will appear in the Content Pane.

IV.A.2. From the Tool Bar

The Tool Bar at the top of the MS Dynamics GP desktop provides two ways to launch task windows: from the menus or from the Tool Bar icons.

The Tool Bar Menus organize tasks into Transactions, Inquiries, Reports, and Cards. Some less frequently used tasks are tied to menus found under the Microsoft Dynamics GP label. These include utilities, routines, customization processes, maintenance functions, et cetera.

Cards are the windows used to build master files. GL accounts are defined in the Account Maintenance window found under Cards → Financial → Accounts. Customers are created, edited, and deleted using the Customer Maintenance window found under Cards → Sales → Customers.

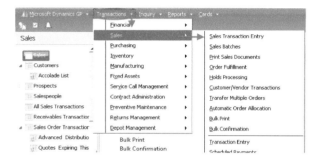

Transactions include the windows that perform business tasks. For example, sales are entered most often using the Sales Transaction Entry window found under Transactions Sales → Sales → Transaction Entry. Other transactions include GL journal Entries, Purchasing, Inventory Adjustments, et cetera.

The Inquiries option provides access to windows that display information about the records stored in MS Dynamics GP. This includes Inventory Inquiries, Financial Account Inquiries, Open Payables or Receivables, et cetera.

The option provides access to a number of printed reports. Like Transactions and Cards, they are organized by module or series, and then type of report. The generation of reports is covered in detail in Chapter VI of this book.

To access a particular task window using the tool bar menus, click on the main category (Cards, et cetera). From the pull down menu that displays, select the module and then the specific task. In some cases, additional menus may be displayed showing groups of like tasks. Reports have an additional grouping. See Chapter VI for information on selecting the proper report from the menus.

The Tool Bar also includes several icons of frequently used tasks. Users can select additional icons to be displayed in this area. To launch the task window associated with an icon, click on the icon. (To customize the list of icons on the Tool Bar, see Chapter XIII.A.)

IV.A.3.   From the Address Bar

While not as easy to use as other methods, task windows can be accessed using the Address Bar. The Address Bar property contains pull down menus. As a selection is made from the current pull down, the next menu level is displayed in the Address Bar. After a selection or two, the Content Pane changes to show the Menu View for the selected module or series.

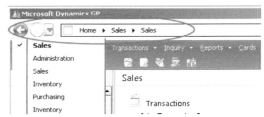

The Navigation Buttons on the Address Bar are more useful. After browsing a few menus, a history of windows viewed is accumulated. Clicking on the Back button returns the user to the prior menu view and clicking on the Next button moves the user back forward in the chain. The chain of views can be viewed by clicking on the pull down arrow to the right of the buttons.

IV.A.4.   From the Home Pane

As discussed earlier, the Home Pane contains a list of scheduled Tasks and Quick Links. The task window for each of these jobs can be opened by simply displaying the Home Pane (click the Home tile in the Navigation Pane) and clicking on the desired task.

When the Home Pane is displayed, the Navigation Explorer contains two folders that can hold additional shortcuts. The system manager can create additional folders if appropriate. These folders can hold shortcuts that will open task windows as well as links to tasks or reports from applications external to MS Dynamics GP. Simply clicking on a shortcut will start the associated application. See Chapter XIII.B. for information on adding Shortcuts to the Navigation Explorer.

IV.A.5.   From the Action Pane

As discussed in Chapter III.E.2.b., the Action Pane contains tasks that can be performed for the records displayed in the associate List View. Launching these task windows involves selecting the appropriate record or records and clicking on the Action icon.

IV.A.6.   From Smartlists

SmartLists are a browsing tool that allows users to view screens of data from the application. The data is presented in a grid format much like viewing a spreadsheet. The user has a number of options that allow the selection of the data to be reviewed. SmartLists are discussed in detail in Chapter V.A. of this manual.

One of the features of SmartLists is the ability to select a record and then select a task to be performed. Like other windows, a GoTo menu is present that offers several options. Maintenance tasks, transaction tasks, reports, et cetera can be found in many of the GoTo menus. One of the functions is defined as the primary function for the current list. Double clicking on one of the displayed rows will open the task window associated with that primary task.

IV.A.7.   From Other Task Windows

Most of the task windows in MS Dynamics GP have links to other windows. These other task windows can be opened by clicking on the appropriate link. Several different link types are available.

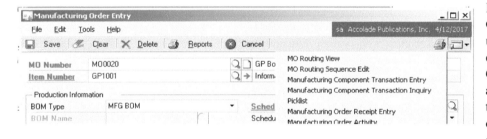

Many windows have a GoTo menu icon (▱▾) usually in the upper right corner of the window. Clicking on this icon opens a pull down menu of other task windows. Clicking on one of the windows listed on the menu will open that window. Information from the current window, if applicable, will be carried to the new window.

Many windows have several hyper-linked field prompts. Hyper-linked field prompts are usually underlined like the Item Number prompt in the above sample. Clicking on a hyper-linked prompt will open a task window. Usually the task window will be a maintenance window for the data in the adjacent field. In the example above, the Item Maintenance window would be opened. The item number from the current window's field will be carried into the new window and information for that data element (an item in this example) will be retrieved in the new task window.

Most windows also have Expansion Arrow icons (➔) that open sub-windows or additional screens. Some even have buttons that again open additional screens associated with the main window.

IV.B.   Common Features

As stated earlier task screens appear in separate windows from the User Desktop. Since each task screen is it's own separate window (including the drill downs from the current task screen), each window carries its own top menu. The typical Windows options of File, Edit, and Help are found along with standard MS Dynamics GP function of Tools.

Two separate menu options appear on the menu bar of the window: Options and Additional.

The File menu option contains, in addition to the standard Windows Close option, options of Add to Shortcuts, Print Setup, and Print. The Add to Shortcuts function will add the current window to the shortcuts list on the Home menu. The Print Setup function allows a user to change the printer selection to be used. Changes made in one window will be carried to other windows in the application. This selection is universal for the workstation. Finally, the Print function opens the same print window opened by clicking on the Printer Icon that appears elsewhere in the window. For example, clicking the Printer Icon on the Sales Transaction Entry window opens the Sales Document Print Options window. Clicking on the Print function in the File menu of the Sales Transaction Entry window also opens the Sales Document Print Options window.

The Edit menu contains the familiar Cut, Copy, Paste, Clear and Select All options as well as the Insert Row and Delete Row work for MS Dynamics GP. These two functions are used to insert rows into scrolling windows or delete a record from one.

The Tools menu contains the Customize, Integrate, Macro, and Resource Description options. The Help menu contains the same functions found on the User Desktop Help menu.

IV.B.1.   Window Icons

A number of icons appear on many of the task windows. Each of these icons has a special function.

Lookup Icon 🔍 -- This icon opens the Lookup windows that allow users to find specific data records. For example, if the icon appears after the Item Number field, a search of inventory items can be performed by clicking this icon. See Chapter V.B. for information on using Lookups

Record Notes Icon ☐ -- This icon opens a Record Notes window that allows additional information to be recorded. The use of Record Notes can be confusing as some windows have many Record Notes icons. See the notes below on Record Notes.

Information Icon ⓘ -- This icon opens a display with additional information on the status of the data in the associated field. For example, when the icon is located in the sales item column, clicking the icon will show how many of the items have already been shipped to the customer.

Expansion Arrow Icon ⇥ -- This icon is seen next to a significant number of fields in MS Dynamics GP. Clicking it opens another screen associated with the current task window where additional information can be entered or reviewed. For example, in the Sales Transaction Entry window, clicking the Expansion icon next to the Customer Number fields opens a window where the customer address information can be reviewed and special ship to addresses entered.

Linked Document Icon ▤ -- This icon usually indicates that another type of document is linked to the current document. For example, in Sales Transaction Entry, it is possible to enter an item to be sold to a customer and then create a Purchase Order to buy that item. The Purchase Order can be linked to the Sales Order. This icon will appear on both documents to signify the existence of the link and allow the user to open the document.

Line Expansion Icon ⊻ -- Many of the windows in MS Dynamics GP show, by default one line of a list of items. This occurs on inquiry windows as well as some transaction entry windows. The Line Expansion icon allows the user to expand the display to show multiple lines for each piece of information.

Delete Line Icon ⌹ -- Highlight a line on a multi-line display and click this icon and the selected line will be deleted.

Insert Line Icon ⌻ -- Highlight an existing line in a multi-line display and click this icon to insert a blank line for new data.

MapPoint Icon ▦ -- Many of the addresses in MS Dynamics GP have this icon present. If the workstation is properly installed, clicking this icon with an address displayed will launch mapping software and display the address' location on a map.

Pull Down Icon ▾ -- This icon usually opens a menu of additional options or a Pull Down menu. Some of the fields must be completed with MS Dynamics GP defined responses. Clicking the Pull down Icon will display a list of valid selections. Choose one to complete the field.

Printer Icon 🖨 -- This icon opens a printer window and allows the user to print a report or list from the current window's information.

Calendar Icon ▦ -- If this icon appears next to a date field, clicking it will open a calendar. The desired date can be picked from this calendar.

Internet Information ⓘ --Primary records for customers, vendors, employees, and inventory items can have an additional group of Internet Information fields associated with them. This would include such things as e-mail addresses, web site addresses, FTP sites, et cetera. This information is accessed by clicking the Internet Information Icon when it is present.

Letter Writing Assistant ▦ -- MS Dynamics GP includes a letter mail merge facility that allows easy generation of letters to customers, vendors, and employees. When the Letter Writing Assistant icon is present in the menu bar of a window, this feature is available. See Chapter XII for information on using the Letter Writing Assistant.

Excel Link ▦ -- Certain List windows allow their data to be exported directly to Excel. When this icon is available, the link can be executed. Select the desired data and click the icon to export everything to Excel.

Word Link ▦ -- This link in the SmartList will export the data shown into a Word Document.

Help ◎ -- This icon opens the Windows Help system for MS Dynamics GP.

GoTo Menu ▭▾ -- This icon opens a short menu of tasks related to the current task window. Clicking this icon and selecting a task will open the new window. Data from the current window will populate the new window where appropriate.

IV.B.2.   OLE/Record Notes

The small "post-it" note (▯) next to many of the fields refer to the presence of Record Notes windows that may hold text notes or OLE objects (Object Linking and Embedding (OLE) is a method for combining data). If the icon is white, there are no notes yet recorded. If the icon is yellow and appears to have lines, then there are notes attached to the field. It is important to pay attention to the field to which the Record Note is attached as most notes are not attached to the current window. Remember, Record Notes support SHARING of data.

The Record Notes entered in the notes window next to the Customer ID for example are associated with the customer. If this window is opened and notes are added, even though the notes are typed into the window opened from the Sales Transaction Entry window, the notes are associated with the customer. When another sales transaction is created for the same customer, the notes entered in this window will be available on the new transaction. When the customer card is opened for this customer, the notes will be there! Any place where customers are used and a Record Note icon appears, the notes entered for the customer on the Sales Transaction Entry window will be displayed. Also, any notes entered for a customer on any window (by using the Record Note Icon next to the Customer ID field) will be available on the Sales Transaction Entry window. These notes are truly shared throughout the application.

The Record Notes icons (☐) located next to other fields work in the same manner. Notes entered through the icon next to the Batch ID will be associated with that batch. Notes entered through the icon next to the Currency ID will be associated with the Currency ID on all documents where that Currency ID is available.

One field, the Document Number field, will hold Record Notes only for this sales document. That is because, like other Record Note icons, the notes entered here belong to the field they are attached to and the master record identified in that field. In this case, the field is the Document Number and thus notes entered here belong to the document.

Make sure, if Record Notes are to be attached ONLY to the document, that those notes are entered in the note pad associated with the document number and not with the Customer ID or any other field.

Generally speaking, Record Notes are not printed on any document. They are available internally by opening the card for the customer or the sales document and viewing the yellow colored Record Note Icons. Modifications to the forms can be made that will allow Record Notes to print on those forms. (See *Confessions of a Dynamics GP Consultant* from Accolade Publications, Inc. for information on printing Record Notes on documents.)

IV.B.3   Comment Selection Fields

Comment selection fields can be found in several different places in MS Dynamics GP. They are used in Sales Order Processing on the order header and associated with each line item. The order header comments are found on the bottom of the Sales Transaction Entry window. Line item comments are found on the Sales Item Detail Entry window (highlight a line item and click the expansion arrow () in the lines header). Comments are also used with purchasing, inventory items, employees, the financial applications, payroll, and project.

Comments are added to data records by using a Comment ID entry field. Permanent comments can be added to and selected from a list. Click on the lookup icon (🔍) next to the Comment ID field and a list of previously recorded comments will be displayed. Selecting one of these comments by its ID will copy the contents of the comment into the Comment Text field.

To view the Comment Text, click on the Expansion arrow icon next to the Comment ID field. The Comment Entry window will open with the comments copied from the selected Comment ID shown. If desired, these comments can be edited. The changes to the comment text will be displayed and/or printed ONLY on the current transaction and not written back to the permanent record of the Comment ID. The next time the same permanent Comment ID is selected, the original comment text will be copied to the new transaction.

To create a new permanent Comment ID, open the Comment ID lookup window by clicking on the lookup icon next to the field. Then, click on the NEW hyper-link near the top of the lookup window. The Comment Setup window will be displayed. Enter the new Comment ID and the text for the comment. Select the Series for the new Comment ID and save the new record.

Comments can be created that are used company wide or only to be used in specific modules. In the Series pull down field of Comment Setup, select the specific series desired. If the comment should be used anywhere comments can be used, select the series Company.

(Any Comment ID can be used at any time. The Series helps users select appropriate comments and limit the selection).

The recorded text for any Comment ID can be edited from this window as well. Simply look up the desired comments, edit the text, and click SAVE. However, once edited, the new comment text will appear on all transactions using the edited ID.

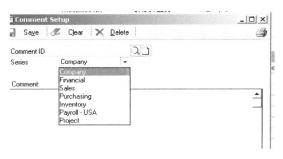

To enter a one time only comment on a transaction, leave the Comment ID field blank and click on the Expansion arrow (➔) icon next to the field. This will open the Comment Entry window. The comment text will be blank. Enter the information to be recorded/printed for this document or item.

IV.B.4. Hyper-Links

Hyper-Links existed in software long before the Internet. They allow a prompt or phrase on one window to link to some other window. MS Dynamics GP makes extensive use of hyper-links. One use of hyper-links, jumping to other windows, was discussed above. The Custom

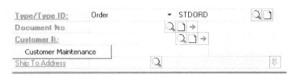

Links function, discussed in Chapter X allows a firm to link some prompts to other functions.

When a hyper-linked prompt is clicked, either a task window will open or a drop down menu will appear. If the menu appears, several different selections are available. Usually the maintenance window for the data next to the prompt is one selection and options defined through Custom Links are the additional selections. This can include images of the employee or item, a link to a web site for the vendor, or the opening of a pre-addressed e-mail template.

IV.B.5. Required Fields

Almost every window in MS Dynamics GP has at least one required field. For example, a user cannot create a new GL Account without at least entering an account number. That account number would be a required field.

Required fields in MS Dynamics GP are highlighted. The highlighting used depends on the settings in the User Preferences setting. Out of the box, required fields have bold black prompts. Typically, we suggest changing the User Preferences to show required fields with bold red prompts. They stand out better!

User Preferences are discussed in Chapter XIII.E.

IV.B.6. Buttons

Some task windows have buttons that open other screens. Generally, the primary window and the additional screens opened using the buttons are related screens that form a window set. For example, the Customer Maintenance window has buttons that open the Customer Options window. The Customer Options Window cannot be opened except from the Customer Maintenance window.

The Address windows are one exception to this rule. Most Address windows (customer addresses, vendor addresses, et cetera) can be opened from a menu selection.

IV.B.7.   Scrolling Buttons

Each window that can be used to lookup data, possibly for a simple inquiry or perhaps for editing can have a set of VCR type scrolling buttons. These are typically located near the bottom of the window.

The buttons are used to move to the next record, the previous record, the first record in the table, or the last record in the table. Several of the windows can move through different paths, stepping either through document numbers, customer ID, dates, et cetera. The pull down menu next to the Scrolling Buttons lets the user select the path. Open the pull down list and select a field. Once a particular field is selected, using the Scrolling Buttons will move through the records in order by the field selected.

IV.B.8.   Window Notes

A special icon usually found in the lower right corner of most windows provides a place where the firm can enter specific notes concerning the use of the window. These notes may be used to instruct users in the proper use of the window, special codes to be used, or anything specific to the firm.

If the note pad is white, there are no notes. If the note pad is yellow, special notes exist.

IMPORTANT: Do not enter notes about the current transaction or record in this note pad. The information entered here will be attached to the window and not the contents of the window. These notes will be available to anyone that opens the window, no matter what data is displayed.

IV.B.9.   AutoComplete List

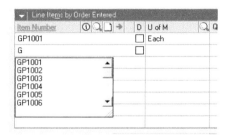

Also called the recently typed entries, MS Dynamics GP maintains a list of the most recent entries in quite a number of fields. When a user begins to type into the same field again, the AutoComplete list is displayed, showing only those entries that match information typed so far.

In the example shown, the user is entering items into the Sales Transaction Entry window into the Items field. Having typed the character "G", a list of all recently entered items starting with "G" are displayed.

Since the list is long, there are scroll bars in the pull down. By typing additional letters, the AutoComplete list will get shorter as fewer recently entered parts are found.

When the desired part number appears in the AutoComplete list, click on it in the AutoComplete list to enter it into the Item Number field.

Caution: Keeping too many entries in the AutoComplete List will slow the loading of the GP windows. The number of items kept in the list is controlled with settings in the User Preferences window. This window is discussed in Chapter XIII.E. later in this manual.

IV.B.10. Right Click Menu Options

Most of the text and numeric fields have been enhanced and now support a right-click menu. This menu offers users the ability to cut and paste information between fields and the clipboard.

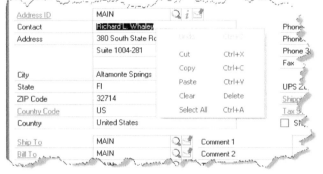

A user can highlight a field and right click, then select the Copy option to copy the data or the Clear option to empty the field.

The user can highlight an empty field once data has been copied to the clipboard, right click, and Paste the data into the field. The associated control keys also work.

IV.C.   Window Formats

While the last few pages have discussed features common to most windows used in MS Dynamics GP, there are a couple of basic windows formats. Knowing when data is saved to the tables and how to delete unnecessary records is important and frequently different between the various types of windows.

IV.C.1.   Card Windows

A simple data entry window like those used to enter inventory items, customers, vendors, GL account numbers, et cetera is referred to as a Card Window. The inventory Item Maintenance window is shown here as an example.

This standard type window contains many of the features described in the prior pages. Notice the hyper-links, the lookup icons ( ), record notes icons ( ), pull down lists ( ), the buttons, et cetera. The user of this system has edited User Preferences to show required fields in BOLD RED.

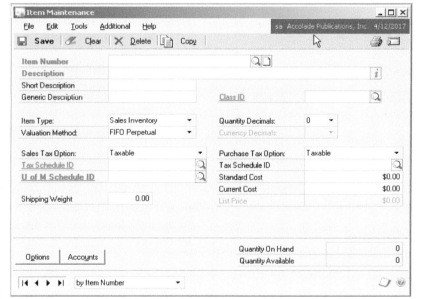

Across the top of the window is a tool bar for the window containing the Save, Clear, Delete, and Copy buttons, as well as the printer ( ) and GoTo menu icons ( ).

These windows are typically used to add, edit, and/or delete master records from the database. That includes inventory items, customers, sales people, vendors, address records, et cetera. The documentation on the individual applications discusses the use of each field on these windows. Generally, however:

To Add a record using this type of window . . .

Enter the necessary information, including all of the required fields. Refer to the specific module's documentation for information on the use of each of the fields.

If any related windows are connected through buttons, check those windows to make sure all of the necessary data has been entered.

Click the Save button to save the information.

To Edit an existing record using this type of window . . .

Locate the field that has a Lookup Icon next to it. Enter the desired Record ID (Customer ID, item number, GL account number, et cetera) and tab out of the field. The Lookup Icon can be clicked to open a search window (See Chapter V.B. for information on using the search windows).

The selected record will be displayed in the window. Edit the record as necessary, making all the desired changes.

Click the Save button to write the modified data back to the tables.

To Delete an existing record using this type of window . . .

Some records require more than this simple deletion process. For example, customer records need to have all transactions completed, posted, moved to history and purged from history before the customer can be deleted. Each application's documentation discusses these types of prerequisites.

Lookup the record to be deleted as described above in the section on Editing. Then click on the Delete button.

NOTE: Deletions are final, there is no un-do option!

Some of these windows have additional functions. In the Item Maintenance window shown, there is a Copy button. The documentation for the individual modules discusses these special function buttons and options.

IV.C.2.   Scrolling List Windows

Some MS Dynamics GP windows have a few fields near the top (and perhaps the bottom) and a scrolling list window embedded within the window. The Sales Transaction Entry window is a good example of this type of window.

The window is referred to as a scrolling list window due to the list control in the middle. While only a few lines are shown, as in this example, many more lines can be entered into the list. Records or lines in the list box can be viewed by scrolling up or down using the scroll bar on the right edge of the control.

Sometimes only one line for each record is shown in the scrolling list. The Line Expansion Arrow (⊗) icon at the far right of the column prompt list will expand the display and show more than one line of information for each record. Clicking the icon again will collapse the display back to a single line display.

Mixed in with the column headers can be additional icons. In the Sales Transaction Entry window, for example, the Information icon (ⓘ), Lookup icon (🔍), Record Note icon (🗋), and the Expansion Arrow icon (→) all are seen next to the Item Number prompt. The functions or windows opened by using these icons apply to the individual items in the Item Number column. For example, place the cursor in an empty Item Number field and click the Lookup icon to open a search window to add a new item to the document. Highlight an existing item and click the Record Note icon to add a note to this item. This note will be attached to the item and will appear any time this particular item is on-screen.

The Information Icon and Expansion Arrow icons open windows with additional fields or information for a specific line in the scrolling list box. Highlight a line in the scrolling window and click on the desired icon to open the extra window.

The Pull Down icon at the left end of the column names line opens a list of options for the scrolling list. Sometimes there will be various different search functions to find items to add to the list, or to find items in the list. In some cases, it will be options to insert or delete lines in the list box (See below for instructions on inserting or deleting lines).

To Add a record using this type of window . . .

Enter the information desired in the top portion of the window.

In the scrolling list area, enter the required information in each line. As each line is completed, it is written to the tables and the cursor falls to the next line. Generally more lines can be added than show in the list by simply continuing data entry.

If the window contains fields below the scrolling list control, enter data into those fields as required by the application.

Click the Save button to record the transaction.

Note that as the top portion of the transaction and each line in the scrolling window is completed, the database is updated. If the transaction is aborted, the partially completed transaction may need to be deleted. Don't just close the window!

To Edit an existing record using this type of window . . .

Locate the field that has a Lookup Icon next to it. Enter the desired Record ID (sales document number, PO number, or journal number) and tab out of the field. The Lookup Icon can be clicked to open a search window (See Chapter V.B. for information on using the search windows).

The selected transaction will be displayed in the window. The detail lines will be displayed in the scrolling list control.

Edit the record as necessary, making all the desired changes. To edit items in the scrolling list box, scroll up or down as necessary to find the item and make the necessary corrections.

To insert a record in the middle of the list, highlight the item that should appear just below the new record and click on the Insert Row icon (⊞). Many Scrolling List windows have an Insert Row option in the Edit menu. This can be used rather than clicking on the Insert Row icon.

To delete an existing row from the scrolling list, highlight the item and click the Delete Row icon (⊟). Many Scrolling List windows have a Delete Row option in the Edit menu. This can be used rather than clicking on the Delete Row icon.

Click the Save button to write the modified data back to the tables.

To Delete an existing record using this type of window . . .

Lookup the transaction as described in the Edit instructions above.

Click the Delete button to delete the entire transaction, including all lines in the transaction.

NOTE: All deletions are final! There is a no un-do option.

IV.C.3.   Insert List Windows

Some windows allow data to be entered in the top portion, like a card window, and then a button is used to Insert (or edit or remove) the data. The Planner Maintenance window is an example of one of these.

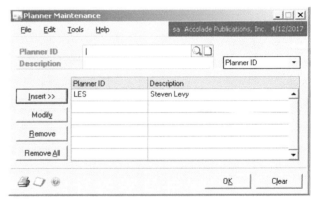

To Add a record using this type of window . . .

Enter data into the fields in the top half of the window. Click the Insert button to save the data. The new data will appear in the List window.

To Edit an existing record using this type of window . . .

Highlight the desired item to be edited in the list window. Click the Modify button. The data will be moved into the fields at the top of the window.

Edit the data as necessary. Click the Modify button again to store the changed data.

To Delete an existing record using this type of window . . .

Highlight the item to be deleted in the list. Click the Remove button.

IV.C.4.   Split Windows

Split windows have two data entry sections. Part of the information is entered on one area and then moved to the other area. The manufacturing Bill of Material Entry window is an example of this type of window.

In this particular example, header information for a parent item is entered on the left side of the window. The right side of the window is used to enter or edit information about the components that are used in the parent item. Completing the data entry for each item places that component in the lower portion of the left half of the window.

This type of window works very closely like a scrolling window.

To Add a parent record using this type of window . . .

Enter the data desired, especially the required fields on the left side of the window.

Add components as desired.

Click the Save button on the left side of the window to save the parent item with all components.

To Add a component record using this type of window . . .

Click the appropriate icon (the application will define this icon) to activate the right side of the window.

Enter the desired information, especially the required fields, for the component.

Click the Add to Tree, Add to Parent, or Save button on the right. The particular application will define the component save button.

Continue adding new components until all desired have been listed on the left side. Following the application's instructions, close the right side of the window and return to the left side.

Click the Save button on the left side of the window to save all changes.

To Edit an existing parent record using this type of window . . .

Locate the field that has a Lookup Icon next to it. Enter the desired Record ID (parent item number, et cetera) and tab out of the field. The Lookup Icon can be clicked to open a search window (See Chapter V.B. for information on using the search windows).

The selected record will be displayed in the window. Edit the record as necessary, making all the desired changes.

Click the Save button to write the modified data back to the tables.

To Edit an existing component record . . .

Lookup the parent item as described above.

Highlight the desired component in the list display at the bottom of the window. The fields on the right side of the window will become active.

Make the desired corrections to the component and click the appropriate save button on the right side (See the application notes).

Click the Save button on the left side to save all changes.

To Delete an existing component record . . .

Open the parent item as described above.

Select the component item in the list display as if it were to be edited.

Click the component delete button (See the application notes).

To Delete an existing parent record using this type of window . . .

Open the parent item as described above.

Click the delete button at the top of the left side of the window.

V. Finding Data

So, the data was entered in the windows with care and the save button clicked. The screen clears out and all the information entered disappears. Faith (or blind hope) says the data was changed. But there will come a time when the data needs to be recovered, either to be used or just to prove it is indeed saved in the tables.

There are several ways to view data in MS Dynamics GP. There are inquiry windows with drill downs, reports that can be printed, and there is the SmartList viewer. Also, almost every window in MS Dynamics GP has a lookup function.

Reports will be discussed in Chapter VI. SmartLists, Lookups, and Inquiries are discussed now.

V.A. SmartList

SmartList is a data browsing function that allows users significant flexibility to generate lists of data from the MS Dynamics GP tables. MS Dynamics GP is delivered with a number of pre-created SmartLists and Favorites crafted from those SmartLists. An optional module, the SmartList Builder allows system managers, power users, and consultants to create additional SmartLists. Users create Favorites.

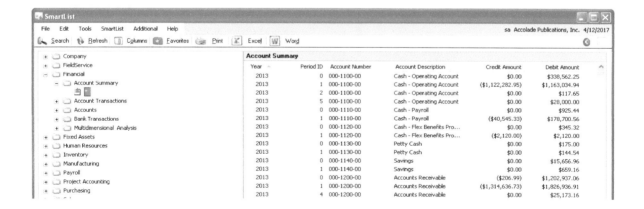

A SmartList is a collection of data rows and columns from a specific set of tables in the MS Dynamics GP application. Opening a SmartList will display the set of rows from the tables and the default columns in an Excel like browser window.

Users can limit the data displayed by entering search criteria. Columns can be added, deleted, or moved in the SmartList to customize the view. Finally, the resulting data can be printed, exported to Excel or Word, or the customized configuration can be saved as a Favorite. Favorites can be opened at any time in the future and a refreshed view of the data will be presented.

V.A.1.   Starting with the Correct List

As was mentioned in the previous paragraphs, MS Dynamics GP comes configured with a number of SmartLists. All lists are selected by opening the SmartList Browser and selecting the correct list. The Smartlist Browser is opened by clicking the SmartList icon ( ) that is normally displayed on the MS Dynamics GP Desktop Tool Bar.

SmartLists are grouped in the browser by module. Expanding the Field Service, Financial, Fixed Assets, Inventory, et cetera, branches of the SmartList Explorer will display several SmartLists for each of the modules. SmartLists use a folder icon just like the branches or groupings do. This is because each SmartList branch can hold a number of Favorite views as well as the default view.

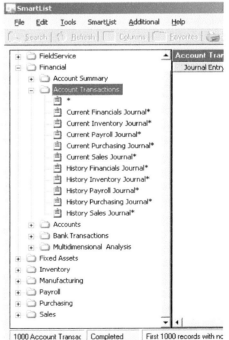

Expanding a SmartList folder will show at least one and usually several clipboard icons, each representing a view of the SmartList data or a Favorite. Each Smartlist has a default view with an asterisk (*) for the Favorite name.

If the SmartList data has been configured and the modified display saved as a Favorite, the Favorite will be listed alphabetically under the original SmartList.

Select the desired SmartList or Favorite by expanding the module branch, locating and expanding the desired SmartList in the module, and then clicking on the desired Favorite. Remember, every SmartList has at least one default (*) SmartList. The data from the selected SmartList Favorite will be displayed in the right panel of the window.

V.A.2.   Entering Search Criteria

To limit the rows displayed in a SmartList to ones that meet specific criteria, click on the Search button in the tool bar of the SmartList display. The Search Criteria window will be displayed.

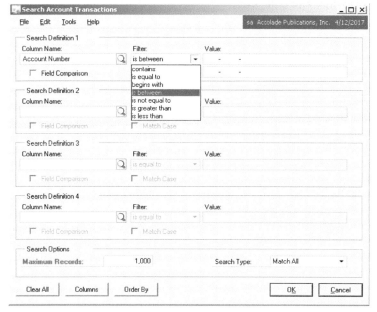

Up to four sets of search criteria (or Search Definitions) can be entered and the type of search can be set to show only those records that meet all of the entered criteria or at least one.

For each Search Definition, the following fields can be entered:

Column Name -- Select a column from those shown on the view. If the data needs to be selected from other columns contained in the tables, add the column to the view before entering the restrictions.

Filter -- Select how data in the column is to be matched to the values. Acceptable criteria include:

> **contains** -- The column must contain the data in the Value field. It is not necessary for the contents of the selected column to start with the data in the Values field.
>
> **is equal to** -- The data in the column must exactly match the data in the Value field.
>
> **begins with** -- The data in the column must begin with the information found in the Value field.
>
> **is between** --Two Value fields will be displayed if this option is selected. The data in the field must be equal to or greater than the first Value field and less than or equal to the second Value field.
>
> **is not equal to** -- Any data in the column selected that does not match exactly the data entered in the Value field will appear on the list.
>
> **is greater than** -- The data in the selected column must be greater than the data entered in the Value field
>
> **is less than** -- The data in the selected column must be less than the data entered in the Value field.

Values -- Enter into this field (or fields if the Filter is "is between") the data values to be matched to the data in the selected column.

Field Comparison -- If this box is checked, the Values field becomes a column selection box. The data in the first selected column will be matched to the data contained in the second selected column based on the Filter selected.

Match Case -- Certain columns selected can have both upper and lower case characters entered. If one of those columns is selected and this check box is marked, a match of upper and lower case characters is required for the data to be selected. If this box is not marked, all data will be treated as if it were upper case in both the column(s) selected and the Value(s) entered.

At the bottom of the Search window are a few additional Search Options:

Maximum Records -- Some tables can contain hundreds of thousands of records. Attempting to show all of those records in a Smart List will not only slow down the workstation but might crash it. This field out-of-the-box is set to 1000 records. It is recommended that the number be lowered to a reasonable quantity such as 100-200.

Search Type -- This defines how multiple Search Definitions will be handled. There are two options:

> **Match All** -- A row must match all of the Search Definitions or it will not be displayed.
> **Match At Least 1** -- If a row matches at least 1 of the Search Definitions, the row will be displayed.

Columns Button -- This button will open the Change Columns Display window. This window is described below.

Order By Button -- This button opens the Select Order By window. In this window, different data columns can be selected that will determine the order that rows are displayed in the view. The columns selected do not need to be displayed in the view. To sequence a view, open this window and select the fields to sort by. Select the major sort first and then any sub-sorts.

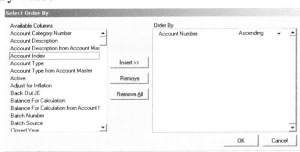

Clear All Button -- As the name implies, clicking this button will clear all entries in the Search window.

Once the search definitions are in as desired, clicking OK on the Search window will close the window and cause the SmartList to redraw the view.

V.A.3.   Adding, Moving, Deleting Columns

Each of the SmartLists delivered with MS Dynamics GP has a pre-defined Favorite with the columns that someone at MicroSoft thought the user would want to see. However, many more columns holding data are available in each SmartList and can be displayed.

To change the columns displayed (either add columns, delete columns, or change their order) click on the Columns button in the tool bar of the SmartList window. The Change Column Display window will open.

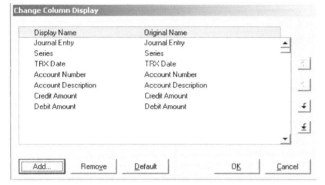

This window shows the current list of columns selected to display in the SmartList view. The columns are listed in the order they will be displayed.

To change the order of the display, highlight a column and use the buttons on the far right of the window to move the selected column up, down, to the top of the list, or to the bottom of the list. The sequence of the columns from top down will define the sequence displayed in the view from left to right.

To delete a column from the view, highlight the column in this window and click the Remove button. The highlighted column will be removed from the list and from the view of data.

To restore the list of columns to the original selections, click the Default button.

To add columns to the the view, click the Add button. This will open the Columns window. Scroll through the list of columns available in

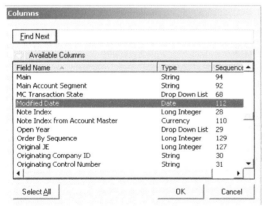

the Columns window. Highlight a column to add to the view and click OK. Multiple columns can be selected at one time using the Shift-Right-Click to select multiple fields one at a time. The Control-Right-Click can be used to mark the beginning and end of a range of columns to add to the view.

When the columns are selected and ordered as desired, click the OK button on the Change Column Display window to close that window, return to the SmartList display, and redraw the data.

V.A.4.　　Creating Favorites

Once the SmartList has been configured to show the desired data, the data can be viewed, it can be exported to Excel or Word (see below), or it can be printed. If the configuration is not saved, then the next time the user needs to see this view, the options will need to be set again, unless the user saves the configuration as a Favorite.

To save the configuration and create a new Favorite, click on the Favorites button on the SmartList window. The Add or Remove Favorites window will open.

Enter a new Name for the Favorite. Two Favorites cannot be saved with the same name. If the original data was configured from the default view, an asterisk (*) will default into the Name field. This must be changed. Enter the desired name.

Open the Visible To field and decide who in the firm should be able to see and use this Favorite. Options include:

> **System** -- Any user in MS Dynamics GP can see/view this Favorite

> **Company** -- If MS Dynamics GP is holding data for more than one company, selecting this option will limit the display to only those users logged into the current company.

> **User Class** -- If users are assigned to classes, then only users in the same class as the person that created the Favorite will be able to view it. For example, if there is a user class Sales Support and one member of that team created a Favorite and saved it with this selection, only members of the Sales Support class can view/use the Favorite.

> **User ID** -- Only the user that created the Favorite can use/view the Favorite.

When the parameters have been set for the Favorite, click the Add button. The Add button actually has two options: Add a Favorite or Add a Favorite and Reminder.

If Add a Favorite is selected, the configurations are saved as a new Favorite in the SmartList Explorer.

If Add a Favorite and Reminder is selected, the configuration is added to the SmartList Explorer and the Custom Reminder window is opened. The top half of the Custom Reminder is already completed with the Name, Category, and Visibility of the new Favorite shown. The triggers that will cause the Reminder to be displayed need to be defined.

Remember, Reminders are those lines that appear on the User's Desktop when certain criteria are met. In the lower portion of the Custom Reminder window, the criteria are defined. There are two options.

Number of Records -- If this option is marked, then by completing two additional fields, the user specifies that the Reminder should appear when the number of records selected by the SmartList Favorite either is equal to, is greater than, is less than, or is not equal to the value listed in the second field. Select the matching criteria and enter a record count.

Total of Column -- If this option is marked, then one of the columns that appears in the SmartList Favorite is selected. A value is entered into the third field and in the second field matching criteria is selected. Based on the selection, if the field total is equal to, is greater than, is less than, or is not equal to the value entered in the last field, the reminder will be displayed.

Only one of the above two options can be selected!

When the parameters are set as desired, click the OK button to save the Favorite and the Reminder!

V.A.5. Exporting to Excel or Word

The SmartList view contains two icons in the tool bar that allow the data selected to be exported easily to either Excel or Word.

Clicking on the Excel button will open a copy of Excel and copy all of the data in the SmartList view window into a new spreadsheet.

Clicking on the Word button will open a copy of Word and copy all of the data in the SmartList view into a new Word document.

Excel and Word must be installed on the user's workstation for these functions to work. Also, the same user that was logged in to the workstation when MS Dynamics GP was installed must be logged in when Word and Excel are loaded to prevent conflicts with rights.

V.B. Lookups

The Lookup icon is probably the most frequently clicked button in any application. It is not enough to store business data in a system like MS Dynamics GP; users expect to find that data when they need it. MS Dynamics GP has a good collection of searches, and with SmartLists included, almost any record in the system can be found using almost any piece of information stored in that record. But the primary searches in MS Dynamics GP sit behind those little Lookup (🔍) icons.

Realizing that not everyone would want to find customers, accounts, inventory items, vendors, or customers solely by ID number or description, Microsoft includes a flexible search system that allows users to define their own additional searches. Several different options are provided, including Advanced Lookups, Custom Sorts, Restricted Lists, and SmartList Favorites.

V.B.1.   Basic Lookup Window

The Lookup window is opened by clicking the Lookup icon from one of the thousands of places that the icon is found. The exact window opened will depend on the the data in the field next to the Lookup Icon. For example, if the Lookup Icon next to an Inventory Item Number field is clicked, the Inventory Item Search window will open. If a Lookup Icon next to a Customer ID field is clicked, the Customers and Prospects Search window will be displayed. The window and the way it operates is the same no matter where it is launched.

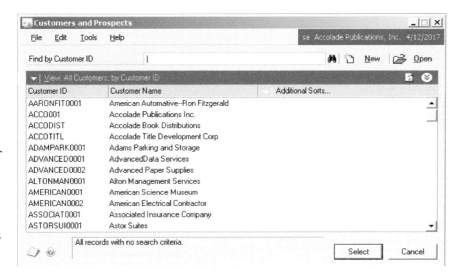

Typically, two columns of data will be displayed. They are usually the ID of the data field and the description. To search for an item by one of these columns, click on the column. The name of the column will appear next to the Find by Customer ID field. For example, if a search for Customers is opened, the default columns are Customer ID and Customer Name. Clicking on the Customer Name column will allow the user to search by the customer's name and change the Find field prompt to read Find by Customer Name.

Type a few characters in the Find field and click the TAB key. The data will be redrawn in the body of the search window to show only records that start with the characters entered. Use the scroll bar on the right side of the window to move the selections and refine the search. Click on the desired line when it can be seen in the search window to select that record. The data will be copied back to the calling window.

V.B.2.   Advanced Search

In the tool bar of the search window, the Advanced Search icon (🔍) can be seen. Clicking this icon will open the Advanced Search window.

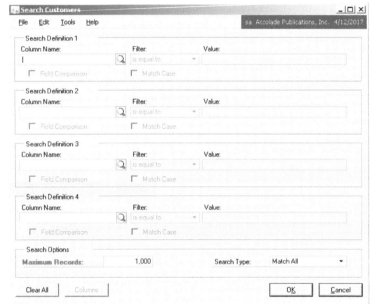

This window allows Search Definitions to be entered exactly as they would be entered when creating searches in SmartLists.

Up to four sets of search criteria (or Search Definitions) can be entered and the type of search can be set to show only those records that meet all of the entered criteria or at least one.

For each Search Definition, the following fields can be entered:

Column Name -- Select a column from those shown.

Filter -- Select how data in the column is to be matched to the values. Acceptable criteria include:

contains -- The column must contain the data in the Value field. It is not necessary for the contents of the selected column to start with the data in the Values field.
is equal to- - The data in the column must exactly match the data in the Value field.
begins with -- The data in the column must begin with the information found in the Value field.
is between --Two Value fields will be displayed if this option is selected. The data in the field must be equal to or greater than the first Value field and less than or equal to the second Value field.

is not equal to -- Any data in the column selected that does not match exactly the data entered in the Value field will appear on the list.

is greater than -- The data in the selected column must be greater than the data entered in the Value field

is less than -- The data in the selected column must be less than the data entered in the Value field.

Values -- Enter into this field (or fields if the Filter is "is between") the data values to be matched to the data in the selected column.

Field Comparison -- If this box is checked, the Values field becomes a column selection box. The data in the first selected column will be matched to the data contained in the second selected column based on the Filter selected.

Match Case -- Certain columns selected can have both upper and lower case characters entered. If one of those columns is selected and this check box is marked, a match of upper and lower case characters is required for the data to be selected. If this box is not marked, all data will be treated as if it were upper case in both the column(s) selected and the Value(s) entered.

At the bottom of the Search window are a few additional Search Options:

Maximum Records -- Some tables can contain hundreds of thousands of records. Attempting to show all of those records will not only slow down the workstation but might crash it. This field out-of-the-box is set to 1000 records. It is recommended that the number be lowered to a reasonable quantity such as 100-200.

Search Type -- This defines how multiple Search Definitions will be handled. There are two options:

Match All -- A row must match all of the Search Definitions or it will not be displayed.

Match At Least 1 -- If a row matches at least 1 of the Search Definitions, the row will be displayed.

Once the criteria is entered as desired, click the OK button. The rows will be re-selected and displayed in the search window.

The power of these additional searches is found in the pull-down menus on the basic lookup window. The down arrow on the left end of the basic look up screen opens the View menu. This menu provides users one of several ways to select the standard sort on the search window as well as providing access to SmartList Favorites and Additional Sorts.

Toward the right of the basic lookup window is the Additional Sorts

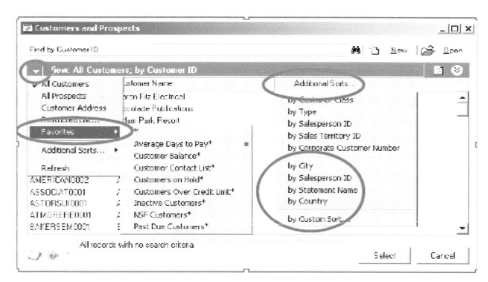

pull-down menu. This menu lists some additional built-in sorts provided with MS Dynamics GP that are available as well as up to four Advanced Lookups defined for the local install by the implementer or support team and access to the Custom Sort menu.

Lets take each of these additional lookups one at a time and learn how to use them.

V.B.3.   Advanced Lookups

Advanced lookups are up to four additional predefined lookups that are defined specifically for the firm by the software implementer or support team and available to all users. Advanced Lookups, once defined are

found in the second section of the Additional Sorts pull-down menu.

To define Advanced Lookups, open the Advanced Lookup Setup window. Select the Lookup Name from the pull-down menu. This defines the places where the advanced lookups will appear. Then in the Sort By Field field, select the desired sorts.

Navigating To Advanced Lookups

Task Bar Menu → Microsoft Dynamics GP → Tools → Setup → Company → Advanced Lookups

The Description for the selected sorts will default to the phrase "by" and the name of the selected field. The Descriptions, however, can be edited to any description desired.

Click Save and the selected sorts will appear in the Additional Sorts pull-down menu of the selected search.

The Advanced Lookups are per company, not per user. Users will need to get together and decide which four options are to be listed in the Additional Sorts list.

V.B.4.   Ad-Hoc Custom Sorts

Also listed in the Additional Sorts column is 'by Custom Sort...'
Selecting this option will open the
Select Order By window. Here
multiple items can be selected
from the Available Columns and
inserted into Order By field. Each
column selected can be sorted
Ascending or Descending by
clicking the pull-down next to the
field and selecting the sort order.

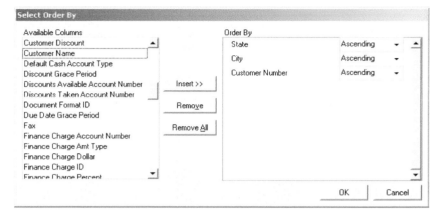

Clicking on the OK button will
close the Select Order By window
and display the customers (or
whatever is being looked up) in
the custom sorting order. This custom sorting order is not saved as an
available sort to be used later. In order to save a custom sorting order,
create a SmartList Favorite.

V.B.5.   SmartList Favorites

By selecting the drop-down arrow in the lookup window, an additional
menu opens with Favorites as a choice. Selecting Favorites will show
the list of SmartList favorites.

The list shown will vary depending on the Lookup Name. For the
Customer Lookup, the list of Favorites under the Customers SmartList
will be displayed. For the Items Lookup, the list of Favorites under the
Items SmartList will be used.

Notice that the software does not open the SmartList window. After
all, users are searching now for a record to display in a window they
have already opened. The data returned by the SmartList Favorite is
displayed in the basic lookup window, ready for the user to click on the
desired record and return information to the selected window.

Additional sorts can easily be added to these lists. Simply open the
SmartList associated with a Lookup Name and add a Favorite to that
SmartList. The next time the lookup is opened, the new Favorite will
be included in the list.

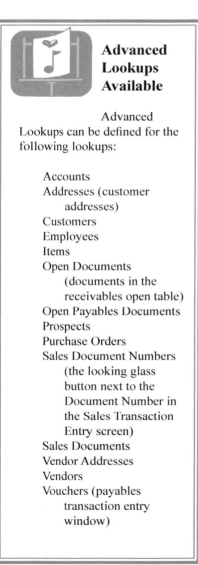

**Advanced
Lookups
Available**

Advanced
Lookups can be defined for the
following lookups:

    Accounts
    Addresses (customer
       addresses)
    Customers
    Employees
    Items
    Open Documents
       (documents in the
       receivables open table)
    Open Payables Documents
    Prospects
    Purchase Orders
    Sales Document Numbers
       (the looking glass
       button next to the
       Document Number in
       the Sales Transaction
       Entry screen)
    Sales Documents
    Vendor Addresses
    Vendors
    Vouchers (payables
       transaction entry
       window)

V.B.6.   Restricted Lists

Selecting Restricted List from the drop down menu opens the Search window below. Here up to four different search criteria can be entered. This is the same window that opens if the Binoculars icon is clicked on in the top of the lookup window.

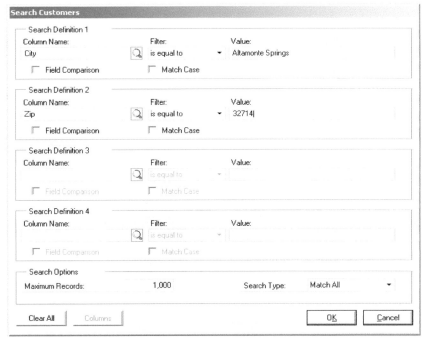

This restriction window works almost exactly like the Search windows in SmartLists. The difference is that the only fields available are the columns found in the default SmartList for the Lookup.

A user can select fields, filters, and the value to be matched. When OK is clicked, the filter is applied to the data in the basic search window and the list of records is restricted to those that match the Search window.

Like the By Custom Sort this restricted list is not saved as an option to select later.

V.B.7. Customizing the Default Lookup

For years, users have been able to open a Lookup window and select from a variety of methods to search for a specific user. The system has allowed for list restrictions to be built, SmartList Favorites to be used, and Additional Sorts. But when the user closed the Lookup, the Lookup reverted to the system defined default view.

Starting with Version 2010, users can now set a Default View in Lookups.

When a user selects one of the alternate views for a lookup, they can also click the Set as Default View option and lock the alternate view in as their preferred search.

Open a Lookup window by clicking on the Lookup icon (🔍) next to the active field. Click on the pull down arrow on the left edge of the scrolling list to show the possible views available. The Restricted List allows a user to create a set of custom restrictions. The Favorites allows the user to display a list of SmartList Favorites. Additional Sorts displays a selection of alternate sorts for the data, including a Custom Sort. Pick the desired view.

The menus will close and the data in the Lookup window will be redrawn to show the data from the selected view.

To make this view the default view, click on the pull down arrow again and click the Set As Default View option. The currently selected view will be locked in as the default view. Whenever this particular lookup window is opened again by this user, the selected view will be the default view for the Lookup.

This function is user specific. Each user can have their own default view for each lookup.

In many lookups, one of the new standard views is to Exclude Inactive.. Selecting this view shows only active customers, active vendors, active employees, et cetera.

See Fun With Lookups in Accolade's *Confessions of a Dynamics GP Consultant* or Lookups in *The Dynamics GP Power User Guidebook* for more information on configuring and using the options in Lookups.

SmartLists Assigned to Lookups

The following SmartLists are associated with the listed lookup. Adding a Favorite to the listed SmartList will add that Favorite to the Lookup Favorites menu.

Lookup Name	SmartList Name
Accounts	Accounts
Addresses	Customer Addresses
Customers	Customers
Employees	Employees
Items	Items
Invoices	none available
Open Documents	Receivables Transactions
Prospects	Prospects
Purchase Orders	Purchase Orders
Sales Document Numbers	Sales Transactions
Vendors	Vendors
Vendor Addresses	Vendor Addresses
Vouchers	Payables Transactioms

V.C. Inquiries and Drill Downs

Using the basic lookup techniques described in the previous pages, a user can open an inquiry screen and look-up data. However, once the data is displayed, drill-downs provide links from the transaction records on screen to their source documents, and their source documents, and theirs, et cetera.

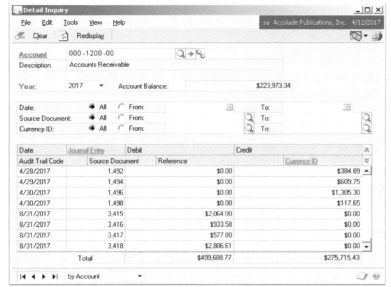

Take a look at the GL Account Detail Inquiry window shown. The accounts receivable account has been selected and transactions are listed.

If the user selects one of those high-lighted transactions and the hyper-linked prompt Journal Entry is clicked, the complete posting journal that generated the highlighted entry will be displayed in the Transaction Entry Zoom window.

In the zoom window, clicking on the hyper linked prompt Source Document will open the original source document in inquiry mode.

In some cases, these drill downs are linked even deeper. From sales history inquiries, customer information, inventory items, or sales tax distributions can be displayed.

V.D. List Views

Then there are the List Panes. List Panes are like SmartLists except more can be done. Not only can a user locate a record and display the details, but in many cases actions can be taken. Actions such as creating a sales transaction for a customer, or placing a purchase order.

The List Views and the Actions are discussed in detail in Chapter III.E.2.

VI. Printing Reports

It would seem like the printing of reports would be a simple matter. MS Dynamics GP, however, scatters reports everywhere. It's almost over done, but none of the reports a user needs are actually hidden or hard to find. If anything, the same report can be found in multiple places.

Accolade's manuals on the various modules list the reports and their locations. We will not be trying to list every report available in the application here. What we do want to cover is how those reports can be printed. There are some things a user needs to know to easily print reports.

Reports and documents can be printed to a variety of locations. Of course, the reports can be routed to the default printer for the work-station. Reports can also be printed to the screen for review. Once a report is displayed on screen, it can simply be closed and forgotten or printed from there.

Reports can also be printed to file. MS Dynamics GP offers several different file formats. If a PDF generator is installed on the workstation, PDFs can be created!

VI.A.   From Reports Menus

Most of the reports found in MS Dynamics GP are found in the Reports section of the Menus. Printing of the reports is very simple if someone else has set up the report options. Otherwise, specific parameters must be defined before the report can be printed.

In the Reports section of the menus, the reports are grouped by type. These types are typically:

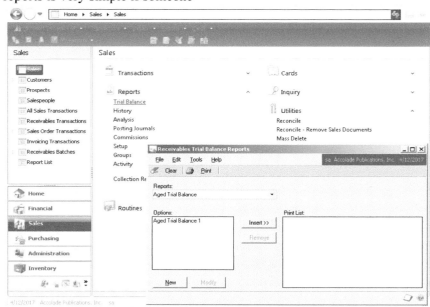

Activity -- A group of reports detailing activity occurring in the current module.

Trial Balance -- Lists, such as a list of a customer's open items, that need to balance to the GL.

History -- Past transactions, such as paid open items.

Analysis -- A variety of reports such as Accounts Due, Period Sales, et cetera.

Posting Journals -- Reprint posting journals using these reports.

Setup -- The setup parameters can be printed using these reports.

Groups -- Several reports, with predefined parameters (called Options) can be grouped together and printed at one time. The user defines the groups and can print all of the reports in the group with one operation.

Clicking on one of the report groups opens a Report Selection window. In this window, reports can be selected by name and a new report option defined or a pre-defined option can be selected and directly printed.

A Report Option is a specific report with pre-defined parameters. Users set the parameters as needed and can then print the report directly or save a new Report Option. Report Options can be easily reprinted once defined.

To create a new Report Option (or run a report without creating an option) . . .

Click on the pull down arrow next to the list of reports (next to the Reports prompt). From the list of reports displayed, select one. Click on the New button to open the Report Options window.

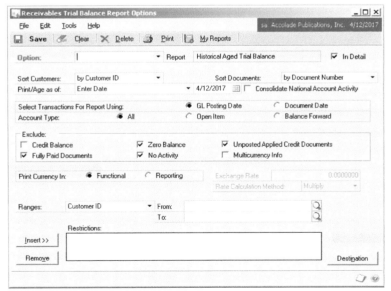

Each report will have different parameters on the Report Options window. After all, it does not make sense to specify a range of customers on an inventory item report. All of the Report Options windows, however, have some common features.

The only common required field is the **Option** name field. If the option is to be saved, a meaningful name should be entered.

If the selected report is simply to be printed and the option parameters deleted, anything can be entered into this field. But it cannot be left blank.

Before saving the option or printing the report, complete the parameters as desired. This might include setting the sort options, the record selection options through the Restrictions, et cetera. Restrictions are entered by selecting a Range (such as by Customer ID, by Customer Name, by Sales Rep, by Zip Code) and then entering a From and To value.

Click the Insert button to add the range to the Restrictions. Several ranges can be entered into the Restrictions box.

For a record to appear on the report, it must match ALL restrictions. For example, if one restriction selects customers in Charleston and a second restriction selects customers in Zip codes from 29701 to 29711, then a customer must be in the city of Charleston AND within the specified Zip range. Customers in Charleston in Zip code 29714 will not appear on the report!

The Destination button appears on all Report Options windows. Use this button to set the default destination for the report. As discussed above, reports can print to screen, to the printer, or to files. In the Report Destination window, a user can select the desired destination or mark the Ask Every Time option. With this option marked, the user can select the destination when the report is run.

In the tool bar of the Report Options window...

Save -- Saves the defined option and parameters under the name specified. Once saved, the report can be run at any time using the same parameters. The option can also be opened, certain parameters (like dates) changed, and the report printed.

Clear -- Clears all parameters from the window.

Delete -- Deletes a previously saved option.

Print -- Executes the option and prints the report as defined.

My Reports -- Adds the report to the user's My Reports List. Click this button and specify a name for the report that will appear on the My Reports List. See Chapter VI.D, for information on printing reports from the My Reports List.

It is not necessary to save the Report Option to print the report. Once the parameters have been entered, simply click the Print button. Once the report has been printed, the Report Options window can be closed without saving.

To Print a Report when an Option is already Defined . . .

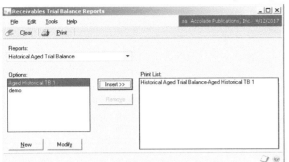

Report Options that have been setup and saved appear in the Reports list in the Options window. To print one or more of these predefined Options, highlight it, click the Insert button to move it to the Print List, and click the Print button. Multiple options can be selected before clicking the Print button.

V.I.B.   *From Other Windows*

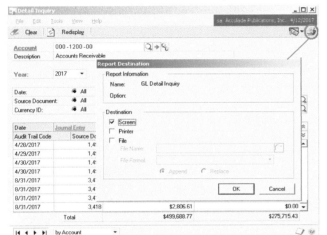

Many of the task windows of MS Dynamics GP have a printer icon (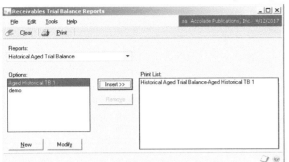) on them. The icon may be in the upper right corner, the lower right or left corner, or buried in the tool bar. But if a printer icon appears on the form, a report of the data in the form can be printed. Click on the icon!

In the example shown, the printer icon appears in the upper right corner of the Detailed Inquiry window. Clicking this icon will print the GL Detail Inquiry report for the selected account. The data that appeared on the inquiry will appear on the report.

When the printer icon is first clicked, the Report Destination window is opened. In other cases, windows that allow the user to select additional data, ranges of information, et cetera may be displayed.

Complete the windows displayed, select the destination for the report, and click OK to print.

V.I.C.   *From Reports Groups*

Report Groups allows several reports to be linked together and printed in one operation. Report groups can be used to print end of month reports, sets of sales reports, et cetera.

Report groups are easy to define and just as easy to print. Before reports can be grouped together, a report option must be defined for the desired report and saved. Once all of the report options are defined, a report group can be created.

To create a report group . . .

Open the Groups window from the Reports section of the module's menu. In the first pull down menu, select the appropriate report group. These groups match the list of groups that appear on the menu such as Trail Balance, History, Analysis, et cetera.

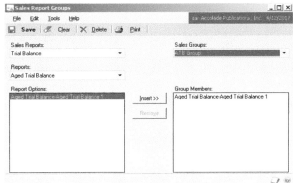

In the second pull down menu, select the report from the group. The defined Report Options for the selected report will appear in the lower window. Select the desired pre-defined option and click the Insert button to add the report to the Group Members.

Repeat this process to select all of the reports needed in the group. Reports can be selected from any menu grouping.

Once all of the desired reports have been selected, click the Save button. A window will open where the user can specify the Group Name. The new group will be added to the Group List.

To Print All the Reports in a Group . . .

Open the Groups window from the Reports section of the module's menu. In the pull down menu on the right side of the window, select the desired group. Click the Print button to print all of the reports in the group.

VI.D. *From My Reports*

The My Reports list contains the most commonly run reports for each user. When a user defines a Report Option, the report can be added to the My Reports list for that user. Users should be careful to only list the most frequently printed reports and not try to list every report they may ever want to run. The less frequently printed reports can always be printed from the report menus.

The My Reports list can be viewed by clicking on the Administration tile in the Navigation Pane and then selecting My Reports from the Navigation Explorer. There is also an icon in the desktop tool bar that will show the list of My Reports.

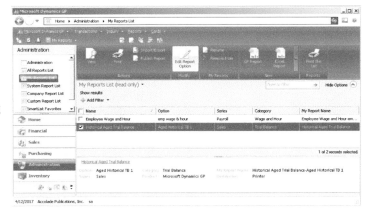

Select the report(s) to be printed from the My Reports list by checking the box to the left of the desired report(s).

It may be necessary to modify some of the parameters for a report. For example, if an Ageing Report is selected, the Age As Of date needs to be set to a reasonable date. Highlight the report and click on the Edit Report Options icon in the Action Pane. The original Report Options window that was used to define the report will be displayed. Any of the parameters can be edited and saved.

When all reports have been selected and possibly modified, print the reports by clicking on the Print button on the Action Pane.

VI.E. *From the Action Pane*

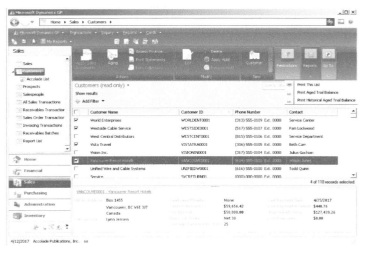

The List Views frequently contain a list of reports in the Action Pane. These reports can be printed with some very specific selection criteria.

The filters in the List View can, as has been discussed earlier, limit the list of items displayed. Customers, inventory items, sales transactions, et cetera, can be limited through filters.

Once a short list of objects has been defined with filters, specific records can be selected by checking the desired boxes in the left most column. Of course, checking the box at the top of the column will mark all of the records.

Now, once the desired lines have been filtered and selected, a report can be picked from the Action Pane and printed. The report will print showing ONLY the records marked.

VI.F. *Printing to The Screen*

When a report is printed to screen, the data that appears on the report is displayed in a Screen Output frame. There are several rules to follow and options available from this display window.

Only one screen output window can be open at a time. If the user tries to print several different reports, the first one will print and the display will be opened. None of the additional reports will print until the first one is closed. When the first one is closed, the second one will display. The third will wait for the second to be closed, et cetera.

Users can scroll up and down through the report to view all of the data. If the report is long, finding specific data can be a challenge. Place the cursor within the report and click Control-F. The Find window will open. Type in a word or phrase and MS Dynamics will attempt to find the phrase entered in the report.

The Print button in the upper left corner of the Screen Output window's tool bar will send the displayed report to the default printer for the workstation.

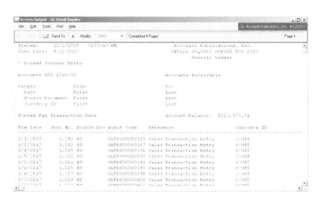

The Send To button will allow the report to be forwarded to an e-mail account if e-mail is properly configured.

The size of the data displayed can be adjusted. Click on the pull down button next to the number displayed on the tool bar and pick a size. This will scale the report on screen.

VI.G. *Other Reporting Tools*

While MS Dynamics GP provides a vast collection of reports, and while these reports can be modified or customized if necessary, a number of firms use one or more additional reporting tools to produce Ad Hoc reports specific to the firm's business requirements.

It will not be possible to detail all of the third party reporting tools or the use of those tools. However, four of the most common tools will be mentioned in the next few pages.

VI.G1. FRx -- Management Reporting Services

FRx (**F**inancial **R**eports E**xt**ender) is a reporting tool designed specifically to produce presentation quality financial reports. Using this tool, the firm can produce a variety of balance sheets, income statements, statements of cash flow, et cetera. Data from multiple firms can be combined into single reports with drill down abilities.

The execution of reports from FRx depends on the installation of the product. Consult with the system administrator for execution instructions.

VI.G.2   SQL Reporting Services

The Microsoft SQL Reporting Services can also be used to build and deploy reports for MS Dynamics GP. This is Microsoft's preferred reporting tool and is now free with MS-SQL.

Again, the actual deployment of the reports is frequently custom to the firm. Consult with the system administrator for instructions on executing these reports if applicable.

Management Reporting Services

Management Reporting Services is a new reporting tool that is replacing FRx. Firms using FRx will be allowed to continue using the tool through Version 2010 while new installations will receive Management Reporting Services.

VI.G.3.   Office Data Connections

Microsoft Dynamics GP includes a collection of Excel based reports tied to MS Dynamics GP data using Office Data Connections or ODC. These Excel based reports can be opened from the Reports List or outside of MS Dynamics GP and refreshed. Unlike Excel dumps created from SmartLists, these reports can be refreshed in Excel to show current information without using a MS Dynamics GP license.

The Excel documents created using these ODC connections can be circulated to users via email or posted in a SharePoint system and made available to other users outside of MS Dynamics GP. Users viewing these Excel documents can refresh the data, getting up-to-date information.

Inside MS Dynamics GP, these reports are found in the Excel Reports list in the Navigation Explorer when the Administration button is selected in the Navigation Pane.

Users can create new reports by either taking one of the provided documents, modifying it as desired, and saving a new document, or they can start with the Connect to New Data Source.odc file and create a completely new report. The Connect to New Data Source.odc file should be found in the Microsoft Office collection of folders. On a standard install, this file can be found at C:\Program Files\Microsoft Office\Office12\1033\DataServices.

VI.G.3.a.   Modifying an Existing Excel Report

1.   Select Administration in the Navigation Pane and Excel Reports in the Navigation Pane Explorer.

2.   Locate the report that is to be modified. The Search Box can be used to assist in the location of the report.

3.   Double Click on the report or mark the check box to the left of the report and click on the View button to open the report.

4.   Modify the report as desired.

5.   Select the Save As option to save a new version of the report. Note that the original documents should be flagged as Read Only to prevent changes from accidentally overwriting the original file.

6.   If SharePoint is in use, the web server will request the user to specify the type of document. "Report" is the appropriate selection for these documents.

7.   The new report should be available in the Excel Reports list. It will be necessary to use the Control/R to redraw the list.

VI.G.3.b.   Create A New Report

1.   Open the Connection to New Data Source.ODC file. It will open in Excel and display the Data Connection Wizard.

2.   Select the ODBC DSN (Yes, the Microsoft SQL Server connection can be used but by using the ODBC DSN, the DSN created for Dynamics GP can be utilized). Click Next.

3.   In the Connect to ODBC Data Source window, select the MS Dynamics GP data source (or the appropriate data source for the MS Dynamics GP installation) and click Next.

4.   The SQL Server Login will be displayed. Enter the appropriate login information for the installation. If a Trusted Role has been defined, the Use Trusted Connection can be checked and the Login ID and Password will not be needed. (Trusted Roles are explained in *Maintaining Dynamics GP* available from leading VARs or at www.AccoladePublications.com.)

5.   The Select Database and Table screen will be displayed. In the Select the Database, pull down and locate the database that contains the desired data tables. The lower portion of the screen will be redrawn to show a list of the Views and Tables contained in the database. Select the desired table and click Next.

6.   In the Save Data Connection File and Finish window, specify a file name, description, and friendly name for the new data connection and click the Finish button.

7.   The ODC will be saved and a Server Login will be displayed (unless a Trusted Role was used). Enter the appropriate login information and click Finish. The data from the selected table will be retrieved and loaded into the Excel page.

8.   Format the Excel sheet as desired and save it. The data connection is read only and any changes made to the data in the sheet are not saved to the MS Dynamics GP tables.

9.   If SharePoint is installed, the report should be filed in the SharePoint folders to be made available to other users through that application.

10.   If SharePoint is not in use, the spreadsheet can be saved in the System or User Level Reports folder as defined in the Reports Library tab of the Reporting Tools Setup. Excel reports placed in these folders will appear in the Excel Reports list in the List Pane when Administration is selected in the Navigation Pane. See below for instructions on setting the locations for storage of reports.

VI.G.3.c.   Where are the Reports Stored?

The Reporting Tools Setup window is used to specify the storage location for Excel based reports. Open the Reporting Tools Setup window, click on the Reports Library tab, and specify the location where Excel Reports should be stored. Note that both a System Level and a User Level path can be specified. Reports stored in the User Level folder will only be available to the local workstation.

If a path has already been entered, do not change the path without discussing these changes with a qualified support consultant or Partner. Changing these addresses can cause other reports already defined to disappear from the Excel Reports List.

VI.G.4.   Crystal Reports

Crystal Reports is another third party report writer that is very popular. Reports written in Crystal can be executed from the Windows desktop or placed as shortcuts in the MS Dynamics GP desktop. See Chapter XIII.B for information on placing Crystal Shortcuts in MS Dynamics GP

VI.H.   Print Documents using Word Templates

Version 2010 allows a selection of business transaction documents to be printed using MS Word templates. The templates can be modified using MS Word 2007 or later. Different templates can be assigned to different companies, different customer/vendor classes, even different customers/vendors.

The report printing system works by first printing the report using the Report Writer defined documents. If template printing is not supported or not supported for the specific document, the Report Writer document or report is sent to the selected output device (Printer, Screen, File, E-mail). If templates are enabled for the document, then the output from the Report Writer is directed to the software that reformats the output by merging it with the appropriate template. Thus while templates can be designed for each of the supported documents, to add a field to a document that is not already on the document will require that field to appear on the Report Writer document as well!

Navigating To Template Configuration Manager

Task Bar Menu → Reports → Template Configuration

VI.H.1.   Enabling Template Use

To enable the template system, the Template Configuration Manager is used.

First, check the Enable Report Templates check box at the bottom of the window to enable the use of the report templates.

Optionally, check the Allow Printing of Standard Report When Template is Available check box. This allows the user to optionally print the standard Report Writer document even if a template is enabled for a specific document. If no template is enabled for a particular business document, the Report Writer version will print whether or not this box is checked.

In the Select Default Templates to Enable pane, select those business documents that will use Word Templates for printing.

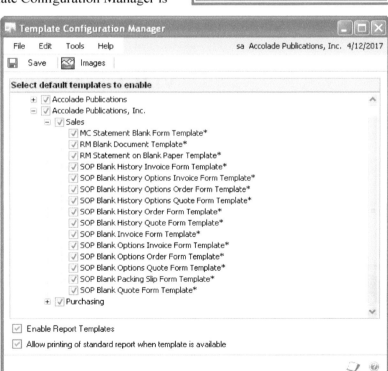

Checking the first box in the explorer, Enable All Templates for all Companies, will mark all business documents in all companies. Beneath the Enable All option, each company is listed. Checking the box in front of a company enables all available business documents for that company. To select specific documents to be printed using the Word Templates, click the plus sign (+) in front of the company to open the explorer.

The next level offers two groups of business documents: sales and purchasing. Checking the box in front of either of these options marks all of the documents in that group. Clicking the plus sign (+) expands the explorer one more level and shows individual documents in each group. Individual documents can be enabled or disabled. Enabling a document instructs the system to use the Word Template for that document when printing the form. Disabling the document instructs the system to use the default Report Writer format.

Mark the appropriate documents as desired. Default templates have been provided and loaded to support each of the forms listed. Modifying or customizing these templates will be discussed below.

In the tool bar of the window is an icon named Images. This opens an Image Assignment window. In this window, each company can be selected one by one, the Green Plus icon (+) clicked, and an image selected. **This feature allows each different company to use a different logo on the documents.**

When the documents have been configured as desired, click the Save button to save changes and close the window.

VI.H.2. Modifying Templates

Templates are modified, new templates are created, defaults designated, special templates assigned to specific customers, vendors, or classes of customers or vendors, templates renamed, and sometimes deleted using the simple but powerful Report Template Maintenance window. This window controls functions described above but uses MS Word 2007 or newer to actually edit the layout and design of the templates. The use of MS Word 2007 will not be discussed in this book other than to point out the launch points built into this window.

Navigating To Modifying Templates

Task Bar Menu → Reports → Template Maintenance

When the Report Template Maintenance window is first launched, the user must select the report to be modified. The report is selected by using the pull down menu in the Report Name field. The report name refers to the MS Dynamics GP Report Writer Report and not the template itself. Default templates are provided for supported documents and, once a Report Writer Report is selected, the default template will be listed.

To manage report templates, open the Report Template Maintenance window. Click on the pull down menu next to Report Name to select the report to be maintained. If any templates have already been modified, they will appear in the pull down list. Otherwise, select the More Reports option and a Reports selection window will open.

Browse to the desired report by first selecting the Product or dictionary that hosts the original version of the report. Then select the appropriate series such as Sales or Purchasing. While all Series are available in this pull down, only business documents for Sales and Purchasing are supported at this time. Select either the Sales or Purchasing series.

Finally, select the status of the reports to be listed. Status options include:

Original -- the unmodified versions of reports provided with the application.

Modified -- copies of the original reports modified by users or the IT Team.

All Reports -- shows both Original and Modified reports.

Once the selections have been made, a list of the supported business documents will be displayed in the Reports pane. Locate the desired report, highlight it, and click the Select button. The Reports window will close the report and the report will be copied back to the Report Name field on the Report Template Maintenance window.

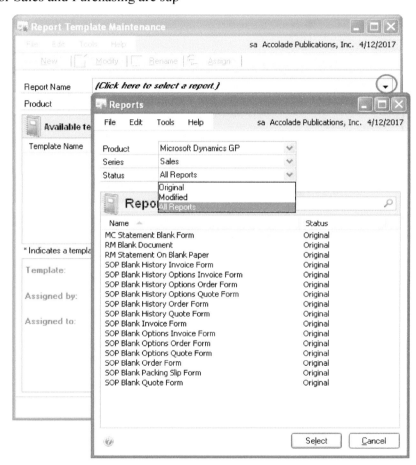

VI.H.3. Copying a Template

The original templates provided with MS Dynamics GP cannot be modified. They must be copied and the copies modified or a new template created. Original templates are indicated with an asterisk (*).

To copy a template or create a new one, click on the New button in the tool bar of the Report Template Maintenance window. The New Template window will open.

Near the top of the New Template window click on one of the options. Select Blank Template to create a new blank template. The user will need to configure the entire document template.

Select From Existing Template to copy an existing template to the new template. This can be a significant shortcut when only a reasonable number of changes are needed. Checking this option activates the Templates pane.

To copy an existing template, select the source template by highlighting it in the Templates list box. At the bottom of the window, enter a new name for it the in the New Template Name field.

Click the Create button at the bottom of the window to create the new template listing. If a template already exists but needs to be added to the list of templates, use the green plus sign (+) icon at the right edge of the top of the Available Templates pane. This opens a browser window that is used to locate the existing template file. This function is useful when templates designed elsewhere need to be installed on a system. Simply load the template files on a share on the server and use the green plus sign to attach the templates to a report name.

The red X on the right edge of the top of the Available Templates list pane deletes a template from the list. Highlight the template entry to be deleted and click on the red X (NOT the one in the upper right corner of the window but the one in the upper right corner of the Available Templates list box.

The Modify icon (✎) in the tool bar is used to launch Word 2007 or newer and modify a selected template. Select the template to be modified by highlighting it in the

Available Templates list box and click on the Modify icon. MS Word will open with the selected template loaded and ready to be modified. Make the desired changes then save the template.

The Rename icon (▯) allows an existing template to be renamed. Highlight the desired template and click the Rename icon. A small window will open that will allow the user to edit the name of the template.

Before a template can be used, it must be assigned to a company. If the new template is to be used for all vendors or customers for the company, it must be selected as the default template for the report. Finally, if the template is to be used only for a select group of customers or vendors, the template must be assigned to the appropriate customers or vendors. This allows, for example, a special invoice format to be assigned to selected customers. The Assign icon (₠) is used to make these assignments.

Click on the Assign icon and a menu appears. Two options are listed: Company and Customer (or Vendor depending on the document's Series). Select Company to assign the template to a company. The Company Assignment window opens.

All of the companies installed and hosted by the MS Dynamics GP application will be listed in the Company Assignment window. Check the boxes in front of the desired companies. The template can then be assigned to individual customers or vendors in the marked companies.

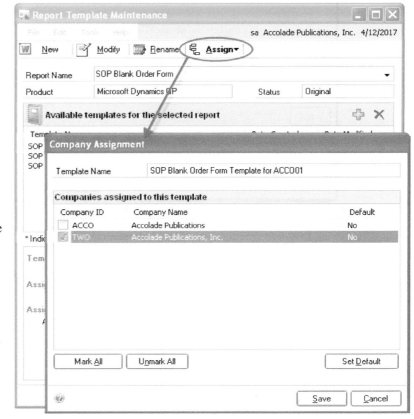

Initially, the default template provided by MS Dynamics serves as the default template for all companies. To change the default template to the current template, highlight a company and click the Set Default button.

A window opens showing all of the templates for the current report. Mark the template to be the default for the report and click Save. The new window will close. If the selected template is the same as the template being assigned, the Default column will change from No to Yes. This makes the selected template the default template for the marked company. When the selected report is printed for any customer or vendor without a specific template assigned, the default template will be used to print the document.

To assign special templates to selected customers or vendors, click on the Assign icon and select Customers from the menu. The Customer Assignment or Vendor Assignment window will open. The explorer in the list box of the window contains two leaves: Customers or Customer Classes (Vendors or Vendor Classes for the Vendor Assignment window).

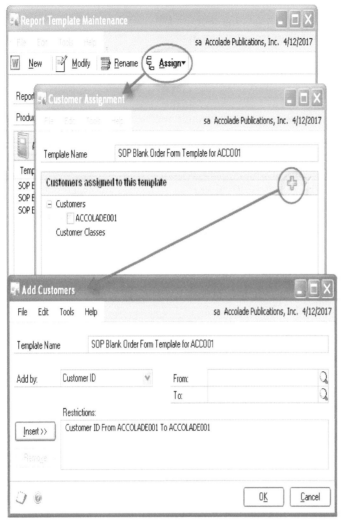

To add customers or vendors to the assignment, click on the Green Icon at the right end of the Customers Assigned list box. The Add Customers (or Add Vendors) window will open.

In the Add By field, select to add customers or vendors either by the Class ID or by the Customer ID (or Vendor ID). In the From and To fields, select a range of customers, vendors, or class IDs. Click the Insert button and then the OK button to add the list to the assignments. Additional assignments can be made if desired.

Once a report template has been assigned to customers or vendors, when the selected document is printed for that customer or vendor, the assigned template will be used rather than the window.

This assignment feature allows special templates to be designed for special customers, vendors, or groups of customers or vendors and automatically used to generate the appropriate documents.

When the template has been modified, edited, created, or assigned as desired, simply close the Report Template Maintenance window. At the time of this writing, there is no clear button. To maintain a different report template, the window must be closed and reopened. Perhaps that will change in a service pack.

VII.   Emailing Documents

One of the most significant features added in Version 2010 is the ability to send selected documents via email to selected customers or vendors. Individual customers or vendors can be flagged for email delivery of Sales Quotes, Orders, Fulfillment Orders, Invoices, Receivables Documents, Purchase Orders, and/or Vendor Remittances.

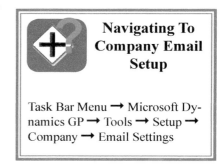

Navigating To Company Email Setup

Task Bar Menu → Microsoft Dynamics GP → Tools → Setup → Company → Email Settings

The process requires a basic setup and some changes to the way customer information is loaded. Let's look at the basic steps.

To enable the emailing of invoices, open the Company E-mail Setup window.

In the Select E-Mail Document Options, select whether e-mails should be sent in the body of the message or as attachments by checking the appropriate box. Note that both boxes can be checked, enabling the selection to be made at the document level as explained later.

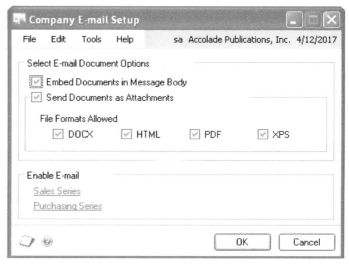

If Send Documents as Attachments is checked, then attachments may be sent in up to four different file formats. Select the desired document formats that may be used. Later, when individual customers are configured, the user will have the option to select one of the allowed File Formats. This series of check boxes only defines the default list of File Formats allowed.

Note: While even PDF files can be edited, it is not recommended that business documents such as Invoices and Purchase Orders be sent as DOCX, or HTML files. These types of files are easy to edit.

Clicking on the Sales Series or Purchasing Series in the Enable E-mail box opens the Sales E-mail Setup or the Purchasing E-Mail Setup respectively. It is assumed that the E-mail Message Setup has been completed before this step is performed. We will discuss the E-Mail Message Setup function shortly. If that step has not been completed, save the Company E-Mail Setup configuration, perform the E-Mail Message Setup, and then return to this step.

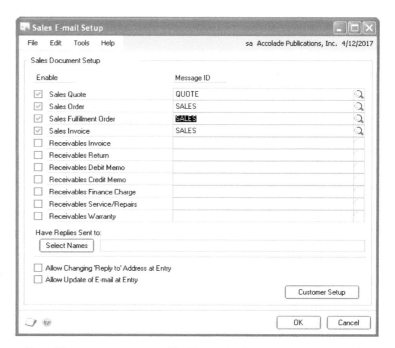

Click on the Sales Series hyperlink in the Enable E-mail box of the Company E-mail Setup window to open the Sales E-mail Setup window.

This window is used to indicate which sales documents can be sent to customers via email. Each customer will be individually flagged for email transmission and on the customer's card, additional parameters can be specified. This window is used to define the default email messages and to indicate which business documents may be sent via email. If a document is not enabled here, it cannot be emailed to a client. If a document is enabled here, it must also be enabled for the customer. Otherwise, a printed copy of the document will be generated.

Check the Sales and Receivables business documents that might be sent to customers via email. Checking a document type enables the Message ID field. (Message IDs are predefined email messages, see below.) The Message IDs selected in this window will be the default Message ID for the document type. Each user can potentially have their own special Message ID as will be explained later.

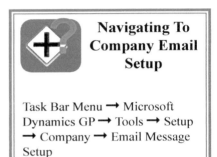

Navigating To Company Email Setup

Task Bar Menu → Microsoft Dynamics GP → Tools → Setup → Company → Email Message Setup

Use the Lookup (🔍) icon to the right of the Message ID field to display a list of available Message IDs. If the desired Message ID does not appear in the list, click the New button on the Lookup window or click the Message ID prompt at the top of this window to open the Message Setup window. (This window can also be opened from the Setup/Company section of the Administrator menu).

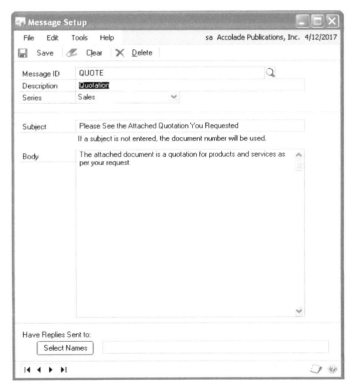

The Message Setup window is used to configure the basic email message that will convey the business document. Each different message is assigned an ID and a Description to help identify the message for maintenance. The Series (Sales or Purchasing) must be selected and the document defined will only be available in the selected services.

Specify a Subject line to appear on the email. If the subject line is left blank, the document number will be plugged in. Of course, when a customer or vendor gets an email with ORD001234 in the subject line, they may just delete it as spam. Enter an appropriate Subject that will pass spam filters (don't use "Here is the information you requested!" for example), and will tell the reader what is contained in the email.

If the business document is being sent as an attachment, it is suggested that at least a short comment be entered into the Body area. This comment will be sent in the body of the email. If the business document is being sent IN the body of the email, it will appear immediately following any text entered in this field.

The business documents that can be emailed can also be generated using the Microsoft Word forms feature described later in this section, providing an attractive emailed business document.

Click on the Purchasing Series hyperlink in the Enable E-mail box of the Company E-mail Setup window to open the Purchasing E-mail Setup window.

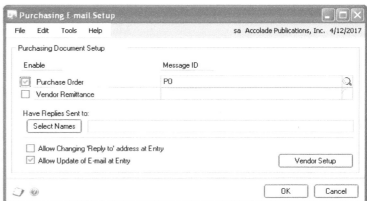

Like the Sales Series E-mail Setup window, this window allows for the selection of default Message IDs to be used to send Purchase Orders or Vendor Remittances via email. Each vendor, however, can have a specific Message ID specified. In the Vendor Maintenance window, click on the E-mail button in the bottom right corner and enter specific Message IDs to be used to send these documents to the selected vendor. If a Message ID is not selected for specific vendors, the documents will be emailed using the Message IDs selected in this window.

The Have Replies Sent To field allows the system manager to define the individual that should normally receive replies to these e-mails. Of course, like the Sales Series, this can be changed for each Message ID.

And then, there is the Allow Changing 'Reply to' address at Entry check box. If this box is checked, the user sending a document via email can edit the Reply To address for the specific email. For example, if several buyers each have specific vendors assigned to them, different Message IDs can be assigned to vendors depending on which buyer works with the vendor. However, if the several vendors all share a common set of vendors, no one reply address can be correct. This will require the enabling of the Reply To address at the time the document is generated.

Just like the Sales E-mail Setup, if a Message ID is needed that does not exist, users can create one on the fly.

For both sales and purchasing, the selections made here are defaults. No other configuration needs to occur to enable the transmission of documents via e-mail. However, some customers or some vendors may have special requirements. This might be a different reply to address, different information in the body of the email or even different formats. Each vendor and customer has, in the maintenance window for the customer or vendor, an E-mail button that opens a window that closely resembles the Sales or Purchasing E-Mail Setup. This window allows special configurations for the selected vendor or customer to be entered.

Information that can be custom configured per customer or vendor include:

- Send Documents as Attachments or Embed Documents in Message Body

- Multiple Attachments per E-mail

- Maximum File Size (many e-mail systems limit the size of incoming attachments).

- The Message ID for the various document types (if a document type is not configured to be e-mailed in the Company Setup, it cannot be configured for an individual customer or vendor)

- The Format to use for the attachment (docx, html, pdf, or xps)

When sending documents as HTML, the MS Dynamics GP Report Writer version of the document will be used. The Microsoft Word Forms Feature is not required for this format.

When documents are sent in DOCX format, the Microsoft Word Forms Feature must be configured. It is not necessary to install MS Word 2007 or newer on the workstation.

When sending documents in PDF or XPS, the MS Word Forms Feature version of the document is used and MS Word 2007 or newer must be installed on the workstation. It is not necessary to install the Adobe PDF Generator software.

When sending business documents by email, make sure to contact the customer and gain their acceptance for the program. Failure to take this step can result in extending the receivables payment cycle.

Customers and vendors are, at the time of this writing, just getting comfortable with emailed business documents. They must also be setup to capture those documents and properly enter them into their systems for processing. If a business document is missed, business is missed.

More and more firms are accepting the electronic transmission of business documents. We recommend contacting the customers and vendors, informing them of the firm's ability and desire to email business documents, getting their approval, and, most importantly, getting the proper email address to be used. Let them know what to expect in the subject line of the messages and ask them to be sure their spam filter software passes the messages through without challenge.

VIII. Posting

Different accounting software packages take different approaches to the processing of transactions. All of the options generally can be reduced to two different schemes: Batch vs. Transactional processing.

In batch processing all transactions are recorded in a set of tables in the system. Reports can be printed, the data can be examined and proofread, and then the batch is posted. Batch processing allows a significant amount of control and manual validation. Information can be entered by junior employees, reviewed by management, and then posted.

As software systems grew in sophistication, much of the management review was assumed by the software. The reduction in errors allowed immediate posting to become a viable option. As well, certain aspects of a business' operation found the delays in processing transactions through batches to be an inconvenience. When inventory is received, for example, sales wants to ship it immediately to those customers that have been waiting. To take the time to validate the receipts against purchase orders, proof the batch of receipts, and then post delays of the shipment of the sales orders.

A second form of transaction processing is immediate transactional processing evolved. With this immediate processing, transactions are posted as soon as they are entered. Each transaction effectively becomes a batch of one and the company relies on the software validations and the ease of correcting transactions to ensure the accuracy of the information.

With transactional posting, inventory receipt transactions update quantities on hand immediately. The GL transactions are created and written to other tables. These transactions can be posted directly through to the trial balance immediately.

Both of these posting schemes, batch and transactional, have their own benefits and risks. Which scheme a firm employs depends on the size of the firm and the controls that are needed. Small businesses, for example, where the owners are personally involved in the operation of the firm and, on a day-to-day basis, enter and post most of the transactions, may not need to print batch reports and review the data. More often, they don't have the time for these extra steps and want simply to receive inventory and print balance sheets.

Larger firms, with stockholders and boards of directors hire teams of accountants to ensure their investments are properly managed. These specialists in accountability like to review all of the financial transactions. For these firms, batch reports are a vital control document, allowing them to certify to the stockholders the proper handling of their investments.

MS Dynamics GP supports both forms of posting. During the implementation of the site, decisions are made concerning the method of posting transactions. Transactions can be processed through batches or immediately using what is referred to as transaction posting. It is also possible to process some transactions immediately and others through batches.

Posting in MS Dynamics GP occurs at a number of well defined points. At each of these posting points, the system can be configured to allow or disallow transactional posting, to require or not to require batch posting. In this manner, an implementer can require all transactions to be recorded in batches, verified, posted, and allow all transactions to be posted immediately, or allow selected transactions immediate posting while writing other information to batches.

Consider, for example, the posting of sales invoices. This process involves the updating of customer accounts and inventory as well as general ledger. In a pure immediate posting environment, the creation of an invoice will end when the user clicks on the post button and all tables, including the general ledger are updated. In a pure batch environment, the creation of the invoice will end when the user saves the invoice into a posting batch. Accounting will then post the batch, updating inventory and the customer tables and creating another batch of transactions to be posted to the general ledger. Other accounting team members will proof this GL batch and post it to the ledger.

A hybrid posting environment, however, will allow inventory and customer tables to be updated immediately while GL transactions are recorded in a batch for accounting to post. As an invoice is recorded, the user clicks on the post button on the sales order entry screen. The first level of posting occurs immediately, updating customer and inventory tables. General ledger transactions, however, are written to a batch file and later proofread and posted by accounting.

Hybrid posting schemes as described above can provide the mid-sized business with a highly efficient form of business processing. Inventory sales and purchases can be posted immediately. Accounts receivable and payables departments can know exactly what amounts are owed by and to the firm. Inventory can be accurate to the minute and accounting can balance and reconcile last month's general ledger while holding this month's transactions in batches waiting for the appropriate time to post.

The scheme that will work best should be a carefully thought out decision. Consult with accounting professionals and with the MS Dynamics GP software implementer or support team before making any changes. If the system is already installed, do not consider making any changes without fully understanding the ramifications and consulting with the appropriate professionals.

Lets take a little more detailed look at how MS Dynamics GP implements these two different posting schemes.

As was said in the previous pages, the MS Dynamics GP accounting system provides several options for the posting of transactions, allowing significant flexibility in the implementation. It is highly recommended that a firm examine each of the options carefully and adopt one of the posting flows as the primary mode of operation, leaving all other options only for exceptional circumstances.

At the transaction level, for example, invoices or purchase receipts for transactions can be saved to a batch as they are created or posted immediately to the sub-ledger level. Depending on the setup options selected during implementation of the software, financial transactions from these sub-ledger postings can write to a GL batch that requires additional posting, or can post directly through to the trial balance.

With two different options at two different points, four different posting paths are available. These are seen in the drawing to the right and described below.

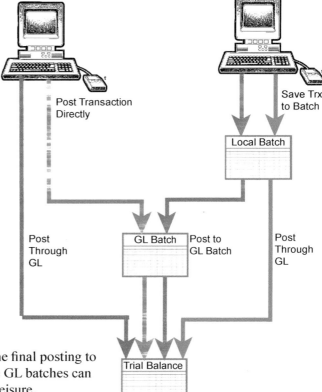

Using a pure batch option (the blue path), transactions are saved to a batch, the subledger batch posted to a GL batch and then the GL batch is posted to the trial balance. Alternately, local transactions can be posted immediately (the red path), skipping the local batch and writing financial transactions directly to the GL batch, requiring one final posting to affect the trial balance. In both of these schemes, The GL batches can then be posted by the accounting department at their leisure.

Of course, complete transaction post-through processing (the brown path) is suggested as a possibility. By setting the posting options to post through and allow immediate posting, transactions would be posted immediately at the source document level and post through completely to the trial balance. In fact, this does NOT occur. Rather, when immediate posting is allowed, a batch is always created at the GL level. This provides a level of control by ensuring that some record of the postings is made prior to hitting the GL.

And finally, transaction documents can be written to a local batch and then posted completely through to the sub-ledgers and GL in one operation (the green path).

The settings that control these posting options can be applied to any of the many posting points found in MS Dynamics GP. Each posting point can be configured individually to allow or disallow immediate posting or to require batch posting. As well, a number of other configuration settings allow the implementer to determine which dates are used during posting, what verifications and/or approvals to require, which reports to print during posting, et cetera.

VIII.A.   Using Transactional Posting

As discussed above, transactional posting occurs when a user clicks the Post button found in the tool bar of many transactional windows. The application needs to be configured for this function to work and a firm may elect not to allow Transactional Posting.

A transaction cannot be assigned to a batch to be posted transactionally. If the transaction is assigned to a batch, an error message will be displayed and the user must remove the batch name from the Batch ID field.

VIII.B.   Using Batch Posting

Batch posting allows users to enter transactions, file them, and post them later. In Sales Order Processing, this is almost a requirement as most sales transactions are entered, shipped in the future, and then turned into invoices and posted. The transaction needs to be stored and batches are the mechanism used. Most of the transactions entered in MS Dynamics GP can be stored in batches until posted.

MS Dynamics GP can actually be configured to require batch posting of transactions and to require batch approvals prior to posting. With batch approvals required, one or a group of users can create transactions and save them into appropriate batches. Another user or smaller group of users will review the batch, approve it, and potentially post the batch.

Batches can provide a significant control mechanism.

Batches must be created before transactions can be stored in them. Batches can be created from the transaction entry window or from the Batch option on the transaction menu. Creating a batch from the transaction itself is usually the preferred method as the source of the batch is defined for the user. Once a batch has been created, it will remain in the system until it is completely posted and deleted. Batches can be reused if desired.

To create a batch from within a transaction, enter a new Batch ID. As the user tabs out of the Batch ID field, the system will ask if the new batch should be created. If the user responds yes, the Batch Entry window will be opened.

To create a new batch from the menu system, open the Batch selection. The Batch Entry window will open. Enter the desired Batch ID.

Several other fields are needed, depending on the type of transactions that will be stored in the batch. Typically an **Origin** field must be completed if the batch is being created from the menus. If the batch is being created from a transaction, the Origin field will already be filled in.

A **Description** field is present in all batches. This can be used to describe the use of the field. It is an optional field.

The **Frequency** of the batch can be set. Most batches are Single Use batches. This means that once all of the transactions are posted properly, the batch will be purged. Other options are available for transactions that need to be posted again and again on a schedule. Options include:

> Weekly
> BiWeekly
> Semimonthly
> Monthly
> Bimonthly
> Quarterly
> Miscellaneous

Batches with a frequency other than Single Use do not get purged after posting. The actual transactions in the batch are retained as well. These batches can be re-posted according to the frequency selected. If the Miscellaneous frequency is selected, a number of **Days to Increment** field becomes active and the user can specify the number of days between posting.

A **Recurring Posting** field is available for the recurring batches as well. This field can be used to set a maximum number of times the transactions in the batch should be posted before they expire.

Some batches have a **Posting Date** field. This allows the user to specify the date transactions will be posted to the General Ledger. Most of the time, this should be today's date. Consult with the accounting department to see if this date needs to be changed.

Generally, there are two pairs of fields that track the number of Transactions in the batch and the Quantity Total. One of the fields in each pair is a system generated total and the second field is available for user entry. Depending on how the system is configured, batch approvals may require a user to count the number of transactions (by actually counting the paperwork) and entering the count and hash total. These values will need to match before the batch can be approved.

If approvals are required, an authorized user must enter their ID and a specially defined password. Batches requiring approval cannot be posted until the approval is entered.

Once a batch has been created and transactions saved to it, the batch can be posted. Posting can be performed one batch at a time or through the Series Posting or Master Posting windows.

To post an individual batch, locate the Batch Entry window for the transactions (see the application documentation). Lookup the Batch ID and verify the information. Click on the Post button.

Typically, one or more reports will print when transactions are posted. This is configured and may be different for each firm. Determine if the firm wants the paper printouts of the reports and print them if appropriate.

VIII.C.   Series / Master Posting

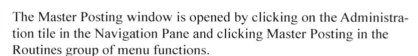

Series or Master Posting allows a user to select several batches and post all of them at one time. The difference between Series and Master Posting is the group of batches that may be posted. Series Posting will show all batches for the selected module or series. If the Series Posting window is opened for the Inventory Series, only inventory batches will be displayed in the list. Master Posting will show all batches for the company and will include batches from inventory, sales, financial, et cetera.

In either the Series or Master Posting window, select the batches to be posted and click the Post button. The selected batches will all be posted one at a time. Configured reports will be printed.

Each series contains a menu option, usually under transactions that opens the Series Post window for that module.

The Master Posting window is opened by clicking on the Administration tile in the Navigation Pane and clicking Master Posting in the Routines group of menu functions.

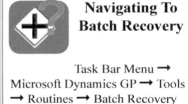

Navigating To Batch Recovery

Task Bar Menu →
Microsoft Dynamics GP → Tools → Routines → Batch Recovery

Address Bar → Administration → Content Pane → Routines → Batch Recovery

Navigation Pane → Administration → Content Pane → Routines → Batch Recovery

VIII.D.   Batch Recovery

So what happens if a batch has problems and the user posts it anyway? Most of the time the batch will be listed in the Batch Recovery. Mark the batch and click continue. If the batch has errors and needs editing, it will simply be returned to the Batches list. Print an edit list of the transactions in the batch. Most errors will be shown there.

If necessary, post the batch again and print all of the reports. In rare cases, a user will need to open each transaction in a batch that will not post and post each transaction one at a time.

IX. Classes

Navigating To Classes

Tools →Setup →*module* →*whatever* Class

Many of the modules (Receivables Management, Inventory, Payables Management, and Payroll) have Class tables. These tables are used to make the creation and update of their respective targets easier. For example, with a Customer Class created, while entering a new customer, a user can simply make the new customer a member of the class and all of the fields specified in the class record are copied into the new customer record.

Classes and their targets (items, customers, vendors, et cetera) are separate records in the database. When a customer is made a member of a class, the information from the class record is copied into the customer record. Changes can be made to the customer record fields after the class information has been copied that only affect the one customer.

The fun begins when classes are edited.

Once a company is running, and customers, items, vendors, employees, et cetera are entered and assigned to classes, someone will find a need to change the contents of a class record. Often, it is the sales rep assigned to groups of customers that is changed. Several different customer classes will have been defined, each referring to different types of clients, each having a different sales rep. When a rep leaves, the company will need to change the rep in all of those customers.

When a class record is edited the system will offer to roll down changes to all records that are a member of the class. Using the example of the sales rep, when the Customer Class record is changed, the new rep is listed, and the record is saved, the system will offer to roll down all changes to the customers that are members of that class.

If a user responds YES to the offer to roll the information down, ALL customer records that are members of the class are updated. The system will not find the customers that had the old rep's name and change just those, it will take all customers that are members of the class and update all records in the class with the new rep's name.

In many cases, a firm will simply need to change the class records to add different information to new records. For example, if an Item Class specified a Cost of Goods Sold account and has been used for months, the firm may want to change the COGS account for new items entered in the class but leave the old items referencing the original account. When the class is changed, responding NO to the offer to roll down the changes will save the changes to the class but not update existing items. New items will have the new information added but existing items remain unchanged.

What, however, happens when a second change is made to a class record and the second change needs to be rolled down?

MS Dynamics GP will only roll down fields that are changed during the current editing session. If other changes to the class were made and not rolled down, making new changes and responding YES to the option to roll down these new changes will cause the target records to be updated by ONLY the currently changed fields in the class.

For example, if the customer classes were changed and the credit limits updated, but these changes were not rolled down, the new limits would be applied to new customers and not to existing clients. Later, if the sales rep was changed on a customer class and this change rolled down, only the new sales rep would be rolled down to the existing customers. The credit limits that were changed earlier would not be rolled down.

It is important to note that not all fields in the target records (the item cards, the customer cards, et cetera) can be changed. For example, once a Unit of Measure Schedule is assigned for an item and the item is used in a transaction, that Schedule cannot be changed. Changing the UOM Schedule on the Item Class and rolling down the changes will not update UOM Schedules on all items.

It is important to know that changing account numbers using classes will not cause any dollars to be moved or GL transactions to be created to re-class any financial balances. For example, if the Inventory Asset Account number for a class of items is changed, any monetary amount already debited to the original asset account will remain in that account after the new account is rolled down to the items. Issues of the item will credit the new account, even though the value of the items issued is still recorded in the original account.

Make sure when account numbers are changed, that any appropriate dollars are identified and GL transactions are manually entered to re-class these amounts if appropriate.

X. Using Custom Links

Imagine opening a sales order, finding that you need to e-mail a question to the customer, and opening your e-mail client with two clicks. Or, while creating a PO, opening the vendor's website with just two clicks. If it takes more than two clicks for these tasks, Custom Links are not being used to their full potential.

Custom Links will allow easy access to customers via e-mail, their web site, and their ftp site, frequently in just two clicks. E-mails to sales reps and vendors can be opened with just two clicks. Access to banking sites to view cleared transactions is just as easy. Verifying shipping information and package progress, finding item information on the firm's website or the vendor's website, and looking up exchange rates is all simple when Custom Links are employed.

With Custom Links, individual checkbooks, credit cards, and currencies can linked to an appropriate web site. Links to the e-mail address, website, ftp site, et cetera for each inventory item, customer, vendor, employee, and sales rep can all be defined. Links to multiple shipping firms' package tracking sites can also be established.

The power to integrate to customers, vendors, banks, and other resources lies hidden in this little menu option.

The links fall into two different groups. Customers, vendors, employees, items, and sales reps form one group, while checkbooks, credit cards, currencies, and exchange rates make up the second group.

Link information for the first group is maintained in the Internet Information Screen. This screen can be reached by clicking on the *i* icon following the customer name, vendor name, Address ID, Employee ID, item number, et cetera fields. This screen contains fields to store e-mail addresses, website addresses (Home Page), and FTP site addresses for each record in the table. Thus for each customer address, separate e-mail, website, and ftp addresses can be stored. The same is true for vendors, employees, items, and sales reps.

For the second group of links, a separate link can be defined for each item. For example, when creating a Checkbook link, the specific checkbook is selected in the Custom Link definition and the specific web site for the bank is entered in the Custom Link definition. This applies to links created for checkbooks, credit cards, currencies, and exchange rates.

Link Fields in the Internet Information Screen

Actually, all of the fields in the Internet Information Screen work exactly the same. The email address, web site address, ftp address, etc. can be placed in any of the hyperlink fields on this screen. The labels can be changed in Setup.

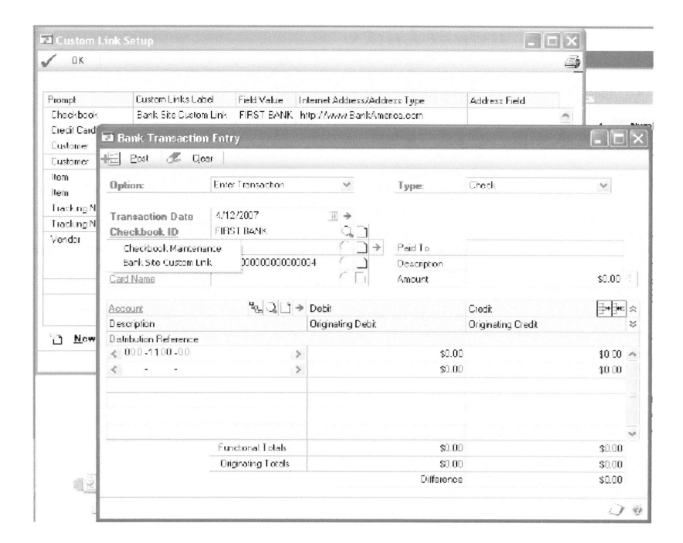

Once defined, Custom Links present themselves for use in a variety of locations. For example, when a checkbook link is created, any place that the Checkbook ID zoom prompt is displayed can be accessed.

In the example above, the Custom Link Setup is shown behind a screen that uses the Checkbook ID. As can be seen here, clicking on the Checkbook ID field opens a drop down list. With a custom link defined, that link is also shown in the drop down list. The Custom Link Label in the Link Setup screen is used as the menu option. The Internet address specified in the Link Setup specifies the web site that will be opened when this link is clicked.

Since there are only a few checkbooks defined for most firms, a checkbook link is defined for each bank. During the creation of the links, the list of banks is presented to the user and the user can only select a valid bank. In the example above, the bank FIRST BANK is seen in both the Link Setup screen and the Checkbook ID field of the transaction.

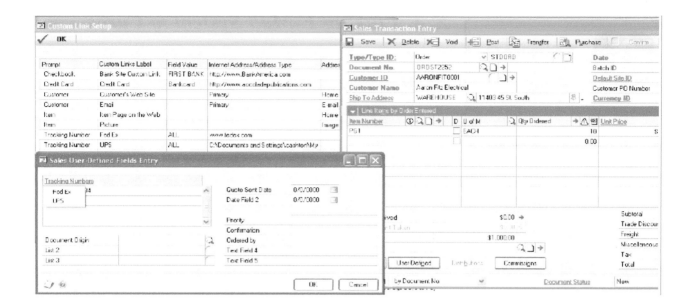

Now look at how the system manages links for the other group: the customers, vendors, items, sales reps, and employees. The Custom Link window describes the link, gives it a name that appears on the menus, and associates the link with a field in the Internet Information window.

When, for example, the prompt Customer ID appears on a screen and a customer number has been specified, the user can click on the prompt and a menu appears. This menu has the standard maintenance screen listed (Customer Maintenance in this example) as well as the Custom Link Labels for any other links defined. In the example above, links are defined for the Customer's Web Site and E-mail.

The addresses for the links is stored in the Internet Information window associated with the master record. In the example above, an e-mail address and web site is defined in the E-mail and Home Page fields of the Internet Information window. The Custom Links for E-mail and Customer's Web Site each point to the E-mail and Home Page fields respectively.

When a menu option is clicked, the system obtains the address associated with the Custom Link and opens the appropriate client, either the default mail client or the default web browser in these cases. The addresses listed in the Internet Information window are fed to the client tasks.

Let's take a look at how a couple of these Custom Links are created.

Multiple Addresses Have Multiple Links

For customers, vendors, and employees each different address record can have a different group of Internet information associated. Each physical address for a customer, for example, may have a different contact person, and thus will need a different e-mail address.

Navigating To Custom Links

Tools → Setup → Company → Custom Links

X.A. Linking E-Mail System to Cards

A custom link will allow a user to click on the Email link and open the firm's email system with the address of the customer already inserted.

To establish the link:

1.   Open Custom Links.

2.   Click on New to open the Create/Modify Custom Link window.

3   For Prompt, select Customer, Vendor, Employee, or Sales Rep.

4.   For Custom Link Label, enter a description for the link. This description will show on the Custom Link Setup screen and on the menus that will launch the link.

5.   Select an address type for customers, employees, and vendors. Separate links can be created for the customer's Primary, Bill To, Ship To, or Statement To address. Vendor links can be established for the Primary, Remit To, Purchase From, or Ship From addresses. For Employees only the Primary address is available.

6.   Select the Address Field that contains (or will contain) the e-mail address. The list of available fields is taken from the Internet Information screen. For this link, the normal address is E-mail.

7.   Save the link.

E-mails can be sent to Customers, Vendors, Employees, and Sales Reps from most of the screens where these individuals are referenced. For example, on the Sales Transaction Entry screen, enter a customer number in that field and then click on the Customer Number prompt. A menu appears that offers access to the Customer Maintenance screen. If a custom link to e-mail the customer exists, that link Label will be displayed. Clicking on the link will open the firm's e-mail client with the e-mail address of the customer filled in.

E-mail addresses held in the Internet Information window must be prefaced with the phrase Mail to. For example, Mailto:RWhaley@AccoladePublications.com

No record is made of the outgoing e-mail in MS Dynamics GP.

FTP and Web Site links are created for Customers, Vendors, Items, Employees, and Vendors in the same manner. The prefix of the Internet address (www or ftp) specifies the type of connection.

X.B. Linking Web Sites

These items are typically linked to the website of the institution that supports the item. Checkbooks and credit cards are tied to the banks that host the account while currencies and exchange rates are tied to sites that make rates available.

The links for these items are carried in the Custom Link record itself. The Internet Information window is NOT used.

To create a link for one of these items:

1.   Open Custom Links.

2.   Click on New to open the Create/Modify Custom Link window.

3   For Prompt, select Checkbook, Credit Card, Currency, or Exchange Rate.

4.   For Custom Link Label, enter a description for the link. This description will show on the Custom Link Setup screen and on the menus that will launch the link.

5.   Enter in the Internet Address field the address of the website to be launched. Websites should be prefaced with http://

6.   Save the link.

Where ever a prompt for one of these items is displayed, after specifying the appropriate Checkbook, Credit Card, Currency, or Exchange Rate, the prompt can be clicked to show a menu offering the defined Custom Links. Clicking on the link will launch the predefined web site.

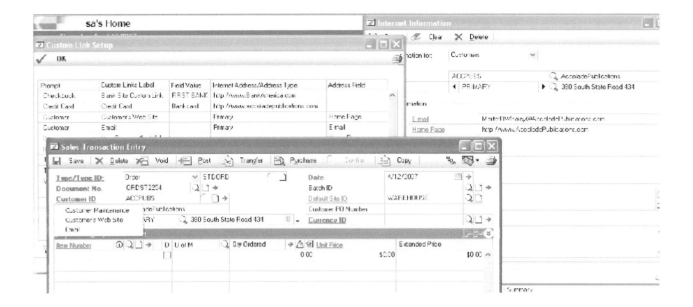

X.C.   *Tracking Links*

Tracking Links are perhaps the most frequently used Custom Links for distribution firms. With tracking links defined, UPS, FedEx, and other carrier tracking numbers can be stored in the Tracking Number fields of the User Defined window on a sales transaction and packages can be tracked with just a couple of clicks.

Tracking Links are built similar to Checkbook links. The Prompt is set to the Tracking Number and the Custom Link Label is set to the phrase that should be displayed on the menu. Usually the Custom Link Label identifies the carrier. The Internet Address for the Custom Link contains the URL of the carrier's tracking screen.

When a tracking number is highlighted in the User Defined Fields and the Tracking Number prompt clicked, a menu showing all of the tracking custom links is displayed. When the appropriate carrier is clicked for the tracking number, that carrier's tracking screen is displayed.

In these links, however, it is necessary to pass the tracking number to the carrier as part of the URL or Internet Address. This is accomplished by inserting some predefined wild cards into the URL. First, however, there is a little trick to obtain the proper URL for the carrier. This trick works for both UPS and FedEx at the time this was written. No telling what changes these firms will make to their sites!

In a web browser, open the carriers tracking site and enter a phoney package tracking number. In the example on the top of the next page, a string of 9's (999999999999999) was used as the package number. Attempt to track this package.

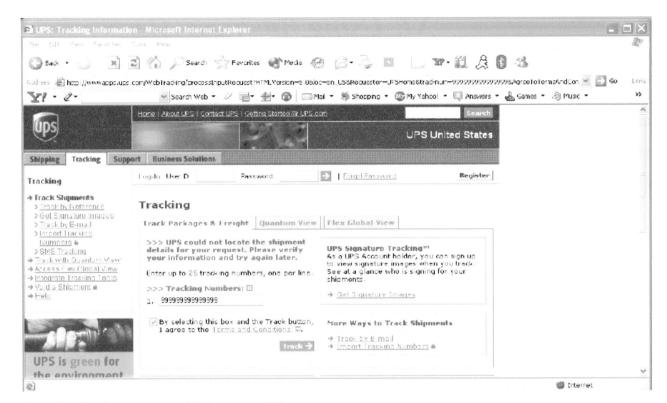

Modified URL or Internet Address for UPS

http://wwwapps.ups.com/WebTracking/processInputRequest?HTMLVersion=5.0&loc=en_US&Requester=
UPSHome&tracknum=%1%&AgreeToTermsAndConditions=yes&ignore=&track.x=29&track.y=11

Of course, the carrier will respond with an error message that the package could not be tracked. However, examine the URL in the browser. This is the URL or Internet address that is needed for the Tracking Custom Link. Highlight the address in the browser, copy it, and paste it into the Custom Link Internet Address field.

One change needs to be made to this address: the package number. Edit the address, remove the phoney package number entered (using all 9's makes it easy to find the package number!), and replace the package number with %1%. This wild card will instruct MS Dynamics GP to replace the %1% with the selected tracking number from the sales transaction.

Do not use the string above for UPS. UPS has different URL strings for different areas. Use the address generated in the Internet Browser to create a Custom Link.

With Tracking Links defined and shipping tracking numbers entered into the sales transactions, customer service teams can easily locate a sales transaction in either the open or history tables, display the transaction, open the User Defined fields window, and track the package in response to customer inquiries. If email links are established, the tracking information can be copied, an email to the customer opened, and the tracking notes e-mailed directly.

XI. Using Business Alerts

Navigating To Business Alerts

Task Bar Menu → Microsoft
Dynamics GP → Tools → Setup
→ System → Business Alerts

Business Alerts provide a mechanism where the system can watch certain user defined critical data points and send a notification to a MS Dynamics GP user or an e-mail listed user when a monitored event occurs. For example, the purchasing manager can be notified when certain key inventory items fall below a specified reorder point. The accounts receivable manager can be notified if a customer account climbs beyond the credit limits established or the controller notified if cash in the bank falls below a defined limit.

Before Business Alerts can be used, two conditions must be checked. First, the SQL Server Agent must be running on the SQL server. Business Alerts create jobs in SQL, and the SQL Server Agent monitors those jobs and triggers them at the appropriate time. If SQL Server Agent is not running, the defined Business Alerts will not work. Secondly, if Business Alerts need to notify users via e-mail, MS-SQL Mail must be configured and running. E-mail notifications are initiated via SQL Mail. Check with the system administrator to ensure these items are properly configured.

XI.A. Creating a Business Alert

Business Alerts are created and edited using the Business Alert Wizard. When the wizard opens, two options are available: Create a New Alert or Modify an Existing Alert.

Selecting Modify an Existing Alert takes the user to the Select Existing Alert window. Here a user can scroll through the list of defined alerts, select the one to be edited, then click Next to open the Define a Business Alert screen. When Modifying an Existing Alert, all of the same screens that are used in Creating a New Alert will be displayed. The only difference is that the information originally selected when the alert was created will be displayed.

On both the Select Existing Alert and Define Business Alert windows, the user is asked to specify the company Database. The database is selected from a pulldown window that contains a list of the valid databases that can be used in Business Alerts (see the next section for adding databases and tables to Business Alerts). The database name is the Company ID that can be found by opening the Company Setup window.

The Business Alert ID is a name the user assigns to the alert. It is a required field. The Description field provides additional space to describe the use of the alert. It is not required but recommended. When the alert is properly named and described, click Next to display the Select Tables window.

The Select Table window allows a user to select the tables that contain the information to be watched and used in the report. For example, the Item Quantity Master table contains the Quantity on Hand field. This field can be watched and an alert raised when the quantity falls below a specified value. In the information emailed to the user, however, it is nice to send not only the Item Number but also the Item Description. The Item Description is maintained in the Item Master table. Thus, both tables are selected for use in the alert.

The table names shown in this window are the Display Names for the tables. To relate the Display Names to the Physical Names or Technical Names, use the Resource Descriptions from the Tools menu.

When all necessary tables have been selected, click on the Next window. If more than one table was selected, the Joining Tables window will be displayed. In this window, the tables must be related.

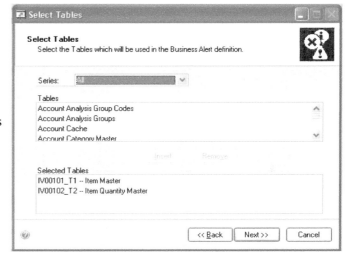

Tables can only be related two at a time. Highlight two tables and the columns from those tables will be displayed in the center portion of the window. Select the fields that are common to both tables and click Insert to add the relationship.

The relationship between the two selected tables must be meaningful to the system. For example, matching the Item Number from the Item Master table to the Item Number in the Item Quantity Master table is a valid relationship. Matching a Customer Number from the Customer Master table to an Item Number in the Item Master table will not create a Customer/Item relationship! The fields selected from the two tables must contain the same data, not just the same type or size of data, but the same data. Unfortunately, the Business Alerts Wizard will not notify a user when an invalid relationship is selected. The Resource Descriptions on the Tools menu can be helpful in matching data types as well as the Dynamics Data Browser, the SQL Enterprise Manager, or the SQL 2005 Management Studio.

If more than two tables were selected, continue building relationships using pairs of tables. Do not create a "circular" reference. For example, if tables 101, 102, and 103 are used in an alert, relate table 101 to table 102, and then relate table 102 to table 103. Do not continue and relate table 103 back to table 101.

The Define Alert Formula window is the next screen to be displayed. Here a user will define an expression. When the expression evaluates to true, then the alert will be sent.

A user can actually type into the Business Alert Formula field in this window. However, to get the syntax and spelling of the field names correct, it is recommended that the short cuts be used. Fields are selected for the expression by picking the appropriate table from the drop down list of selected tables and then a Column Name is selected.

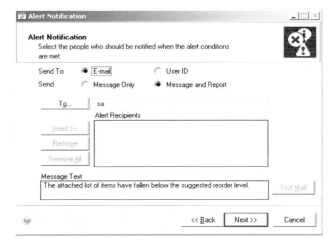

Click on the Add Column button to place the proper column name in the expression. Click on an operator button to insert the desired operator. To insert a constant, type the value into the Constant field and click on the Add Constant button.

Column Names listed are the field descriptive names from the Resource Descriptions under the Tools menu. When shown in the Business Alert Formula, there will be a combination of the table physical name, the sequence number of the table in the alert definition, and the physical name of the field.

The expression must evaluate to either True or False. For example Qty On Hand < 5 will be True if the quantity on hand field value is less than 5. Otherwise the expression will evaluate to False.

When the expression is completed, click Next to open the Alert Notification window. Using this window, an alert can be used to send an e-mail to a list of users or to create a task that will appear in a group of user's task lists. Select the E-Mail radio button to use e-mail addresses to send alerts. Note that SQL-Mail must be functional on the server for this option to work.

Select the User ID radio button to send alerts as tasks assigned to MS Dynamics GP Users.

Use the To field to identify users. The email address or User ID can be typed into the field or the To button can be clicked to open a list of Dynamics GP users or the email address book. Once a User ID or email is entered into the To field, clicking Insert will add the ID to the list of Alert Recipients. Multiple users or email addresses may also be listed.

If the User ID is being used to create a task for users, only the message entered into the Message Text field will be sent to the user. If an email is being used to deliver the alert, an optional report can be attached to the email. Click the Message and Report button to attach a report to the emails.

When the user clicks Next with the Message and Report selected, the Select Report Columns window is displayed. Here the user can select fields to appear on the report from the available tables. Specify a table, highlight a field, and click Insert to add a column to the report. Only simple reports containing lists of fields can be created. When the report field list is as desired, click Next to open the Report Sorting Options.

Select the fields that will be used to sort the records selected for the report. Then click Next to open the Schedule Alert window.

If the alert does not contain a report (Message Only was selected), this screen will be displayed after the Alert Notification window.

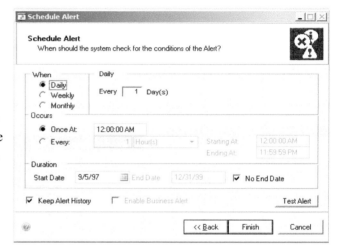

Specify on the Schedule Alert window when the system should check to see if the conditions of the alert are true. Several options are available to allow considerable flexibility in scheduling. Alerts can fire daily, weekly, or monthly, every several hours, days, several weeks, or every several months. The exact item of day can be specified as well as a start and end date for the alert.

When the alert is complete, click the Finish button.

Alerts create jobs in MS-SQL. For the alerts to work, the SQL Server Agent must be running. This is the tasks that periodically checks the jobs to see if there is anything to do.

Also, if e-mails are to be used to notify users when an alert condition is true, SQL mail must be setup and running.

XII. Letter Writing Assistant

The Letter Writing Assistant is a feature that allows users to easily print form letters for Customers, Collection Actions, Vendors, Employees, Employee Benefits, and Deductions. The link to the Letter Writing Assistant is found in a number of windows such as the Customer Maintenance window, et cetera. It appears on the menu bar of the window as a Word Icon (W). If the Letter Writing Assistant letters need to be in a shared directory, the Dex.ini file needs to be modified. The system administrator will need to make these modifications.

The Letter Writing Assistant allows users to create and edit letter templates as well as generate the letters for distribution.

XII.A. Maintaining Letters

To open the Letter Maintenance tools for the Letter Writing Assistant, locate a window with the Letter Writing Assistant icon (W), click on the down arrow to the right of the icon, and select Letter Maintenance.

The **Select a Letter Category** allows the user to maintain letters for Customers, Collections, Vendors, Employees, and Employee Benefits. To edit customer letters, select Customer.

Select the desired function. Options include Create a New Letter, Edit an Existing Letter, Delete a Letter, and Rename Existing Letter.

XII A.1. To Create a New Letter

Select the Create a New Letter from the What Would You Like To Do? box. Two options are displayed in the window to the right: Start with a Blank Document or Start with an Existing Word Document and click the Next button.

Select one of the options. The system will ask for the name of the existing or new document and then open Word. A letter writing tool bar will be displayed in Word containing fields that may be added to the document.

Edit the document as desired. Use the letter writing tool bar to insert fields from MS Dynamics GP. When the letter is complete, save the document as a Word Template in the common directory.

XII. A.2. To Edit an Existing Letter

Select the Edit An Existing Letter option from the What Would You Like To Do? box. A list of existing letters will be displayed in the window to the right. Select the document to be edited and click Next.

Word will open with the selected letter displayed. A letter writing tool bar will be displayed in Word containing fields that may be added to the document.

Edit the document as desired. Use the letter writing tool bar to insert fields from MS Dynamics GP as desired. When the letter is complete, save the document as a Word Template in the common directory for company letters.

XII.A.3. To Delete a Letter

Select the Delete An Existing Letter option from the What Would You Like To Do? box. A list of existing letters will be displayed in the window to the right. Select the document to be Deleted.

When the Next button is clicked, the system will confirm the users plans to delete the letter. Click Yes to delete the letter.

XII.A.4. To Rename an Existing Letter

Select the Rename An Existing Letter option from the What Would You Like To Do? box. A list of existing letters will be displayed in the window. Select the document to be renamed and click the Next button.

When the Next button is clicked, the system will open a window allowing the user to enter the new Document Name. Enter the name and click OK to save the letter with the new name.

Where are Letters Stored?

The DEX.INI file contains a line that starts "Letters Directory=..." and contains the path to the folder where letters are stored. All of the workstations should point to a common share on the server, allowing letters created on one workstation to be printed from another.

Macros and Security

In some cases, security in Word may be set to disable the use of Macros. Consult the Word documentation for information on enabling Macros. In some cases, security in Word may be set to disable the use of Macros. Consult the Word documentation for information on enabling Macros.

XII.B.   *Generating Letters*

The Letter Writing Assistant can be used to generate a form letter for a selected customer, vendor, or employee or a range of accounts. Once the template letters have been created as described above, the Prepare a Letter function will perform a mail merge of a selected range of accounts with a selected letter.

To generate a letter, open the Prepare a Letter option of the Letter Writing Assistant. From, for example, the Customer Summary window, click on the Letter Writing Assistant icon (W) and select either Prepare a Collection Letter or Prepare a Customer Letter. Different groups of letters and letter preparation options are displayed depending on the selection made.

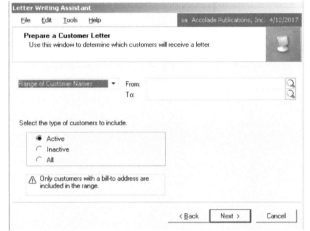

To Print Customer Letters . . .

The Letter Writing Assistant walks the user through a series of windows. The exact sequence of windows will vary depending on how the Letter Writing Assistant is started. For example, if the Assistant is started from the Customer Summary window with a specific customer selected, the Assistant expects that a letter needs to be prepared for that customer only. If the Letter Writing Assistant is started with the Customer Summary window blank (hit the Clear button) then the Assistant allows the user to select a range of customers.

If a range of customers needs to be selected, use the pull down list box to specify how the customers are to be selected. Ranges of Customer Names or Customer IDs can be selected. Also, a Smartlist Favorite from the Customer Smartlist can be selected and the accounts selected via that favorite can be used. Of course, an All Customers option can be selected.

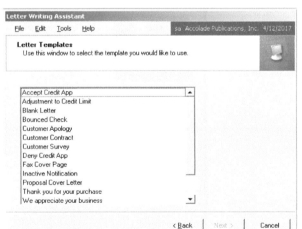

If one of the range selections is made, enter the From and To Customer Name or Customer ID. If the Smartlist selection is taken, a list of Favorites is displayed. Select the desired Favorite.

When the Next button is clicked, the list of Letter Templates is displayed. Select the desired letter from the list and click Next.

If the Letter Writing Assistant was opened with a single customer displayed in the home screen (such as the Customer Summary window), the application will assume that a letter is to be generated only for that one customer.

Select the desired letter by highlighting it and click the Next button.

The Letter Writing Assistant will display a proof list of the customers pre-selected to receive a copy of the letter. If the Assistant was opened from a window with a customer displayed, only one customer will appear in the list. If the Assistant went through the range selection process, a longer list of customers taken from the range selection will be displayed.

All customers in the window will be marked. The user has buttons to Unmark All or Mark All of the customers displayed. Also, the user can select or un-select customers one at a time by checking or un-checking the customers one at a time.

Note that the Letter Writing Assistant can only send letters to customers with a Bill To Address. Customers without a Bill To Address specified in the Customer Card will not be selected or available for selection.

When the desired accounts have been selected/marked, click the Next button. The Completing the Letter Writing Assistant window will open.

Several fields appear on the Completing window that are not contained in the MS Dynamics GP database but can be used on letters. This includes the name of the sender, the sender's title, phone number, fax number, and e-mail address. Complete these fields as desired even if they are not used in the current letter. Once they are completed, the Letter Writing Assistant will remember them. If necessary, they can be changed before printing the next batch of letters.

Clicking Finish on the Completing window will prompt MicroSoft Word to open the template letter, and merge that template with the selected list of customers. The letters can be printed and mailed to the customer(s).

To Print Collection Letters . . .

Collection letters are generated in much the same manner as standard customer letters. A different group of letter templates is offered, of course, and an additional selection criteria is available.

Aged Balances can be used as part of the selection criteria for collection letters. Mark the ageing buckets and any customer with balances due in the marked buckets will be selected. In the example, the 91-120 Days bucket is marked. ONLY customers that have a balance due in this bucket will be selected. To select customers that have a balance due that is 91 days or older, mark all of the boxes from the 91-120 Days down.

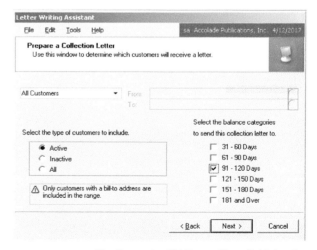

XIII. Modifying The Desktop

There are a number of tools that can be used to make extensive modifications to MS Dynamics GP. In the next few pages we are going to look ONLY at a few built in features that will allow the user to customize their desktop without writing special code. These configuration options are simple to use and very helpful in tailoring the desktop to the user's specific job.

XIII.A.   Tool Bars, Menus, & Navigation Pane

The tool bars and menus in MS Dynamics GP are user specific. Tool bars and some menu items can be easily edited. Users can select from a variety of tool bars to display and even create customized tool bars. As well, some of the items on user's menus can be edited to give them a more meaningful name.

The Tool Bar menu (Layout Icon (▯) → Toolbars) allows users to select the specific tool bars to be displayed. The number of tool bars available depends on the products installed on a system, but all available tool bars are listed here. Simply click on the desired tool bar and it will be added to the MS Dynamics GP's Tool Bar. The Custom Tool Bar listed in the group of available tool bars allows users to build their own collection of tasks.

Tool bar and menu changes are made from the Tool Bar Customization window (View → Toolbars → Customize). The pull-down list at the top of the Tool Bar Customization window allows the user to select the tool bar to be edited. All of the tool bars currently being displayed are marked with an asterisk (*).

Selecting a tool bar and clicking the Add button opens the Add Command window. Here, users can browse to a menu function and add that option to the selected tool bar. The option added can be individual functions or menus.

The Modify Selection button on the Tool Bar Customization window allows users to change the name of the tasks selected. These name changes are also reflected on the original menus. For example, if a user selects the Purchasing tool bar, then highlights the Transaction Entry option and changes the name to "Voucher Entry", the item on the purchasing transactions menu will also read Voucher Entry rather than Transaction Entry. This function provides users with more meaningful menu item names.

Other changes that can be made include the icon that appears on the tool bar as well as the style of display. From the Modify Selection pull down menu, select Change Button Icon. The Change Icon window will appear. Click on the desired icon and click the OK button.

The user can also change the display on the tool bar with options to show the image only, text only, or the image and text. Divider lines can be inserted if desired to group icons.

The Navigation Pane can be edited by clicking on the Configure (⁊) button found in the bottom right corner of the Navigation Pane. The configure menu offers four options: Show More Buttons, Show Fewer Buttons, Add, and Navigation Pane Options.

The Show More Buttons option increases the size of the Navigation Pane. This can also be accomplished by dragging the bar that separates the Navigation Pane from the Navigation Explorer upward.

The Show Less Buttons option decreases the size of the Navigation Pane. This can also be accomplished by dragging the bar that separates the Navigation Pane from the Navigation Explorer downward.

The Add option allows Shortcuts to be added to the Home Navigation Explorer tab. Shortcuts are discussed in Chapter XIII.B. below.

The Navigation Pane Options selection opens the Navigation Pane Options window. This window contains a list of the tiles that may appear in the Navigation Pane. A checkbox appears to the left of each series name. Only the checked series/modules will appear in the user's Navigation Pane. Also, an option can be selected from the list and the Move Up or Move Down button clicked to change the order of the tiles.

XIII.B.   *Shortcuts*

While the tool bar functions described above can add icons to the MS Dynamics GP Tool Bar, the Add Shortcuts functions allow shortcuts to be added to the Navigation Explorer Bar. Like the tool bar icons, the shortcuts allow a task window to be opened with a single click.

Unlike toolbars, however, shortcuts can open MS Dynamics GP windows, SmartLists, play recorded Macros, open web pages, even run external programs (like Crystal Reports). Folders can be created in the Explorer where shortcuts can be grouped by function.

Shortcuts can be added to the Navigation Explorer from two different locations. The user can click on the Configure button on the lower right corner of the Navigation Pane and from the menu displayed, select Add. The user can also place the cursor in the Navigation Explorer, right

click and click on the Add option on that menu. A menu of Add Options will be displayed.

XIII.B.1. Add a Window Shortcut

There are two ways to add a task window to the Navigation Explorer, from the Add Window Shortcut window or from the actual task window itself.

If the Add Window option is selected from the configure menu, the Add Window Shortcut window opens. This window contains a field where a name for the shortcut can be entered and an explorer of Available Windows. The user should first enter a name for the new shortcut. In the explorer, click on the group of windows to expand the list. Continue expanding the list until individual tasks are shown and highlight the desired task.

At the bottom of the Add Window Shortcut window is a Keyboard Shortcut pull down list. Selecting a keystroke from this list will enable the user to launch this task by simply clicking on the selected key. For example, if the Item Maintenance window is selected in the Available Windows field and the F10 key is selected in the Keyboard Shortcuts, once the shortcut is Added, the user can simply click the F10 key to open the Inventory Maintenance window.

From any MS Dynamics GP window, the user can always click on the File option in the menu bar and select the Add to Shortcuts option. This function has no configuration options but will add the current window to the list of shortcuts in the Navigation Explorer immediately. However, once the shortcut is in the Explorer, the user can right click on the shortcut, select the Properties option, and set the shortcut name and Keyboard Shortcut.

XIII.B.2. Add a SmartList Shortcut

SmartList shortcuts are added in the same manner as window shortcuts. The difference is that a SmartList Favorite is tied to the shortcut and opened when the shortcut is clicked.

Just like shortcuts for windows, the user can enter a Name for the shortcut, select the desired Favorite from an Explorer list, and associate a Keyboard Shortcut with the Favorite.

Shortcut File Locations

The targets of Macro and External shortcuts should be stored on the firm's network in a shared folder that is mapped to every workstation using the same drive letter. If a user creates a shortcut that points to D:\Reports\MyReport.crl and, from other workstations the report is on the E: drive, the shortcut will not work properly.

Discuss the storage locations for tasks used in shortcuts with the system administrator to avoid problems.

XIII.B.3. Add a Macro Shortcut

Creating a Macro Shortcut works a bit different. Since users record their own macros and store the files anywhere on the system, it is not possible to display an explorer of pre-recorded macros.

Just to be clear, a macro is a series of recorded keystrokes that the user may need to repeat frequently. For example, if the user is creating a batch of parts and most of the information is the same for each item, the user can record a macro that will enter all of the identical values in the fields.

See Chapter XIV.A. for information on recording Macros.

To create a shortcut for a macro, select the Add a Macro option from the configuration menu. The Add Macro Shortcut window will open.

Enter a name for the macro. Then use the Browse button to locate the pre-recorded macro file. Macro files typically end with a MAC extension. If desired, select a Keyboard Shortcut and click Add to record the shortcut.

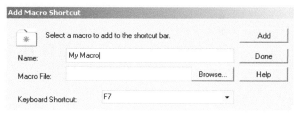

XIII.B.4. Add a Web Page Shortcut

A shortcut to open an Internet or Intranet web page is created the same way that Macro Shortcuts are created. The window is slightly different in that it requests the user enter the address of the target web page.

XIII.B.5. Add an External Shortcut

A shortcut to run an external program is again created the same way that Macro Shortcuts are created. There is a separate selection from the configuration menu since the executable program name and path must be entered rather than a macro file name. Make sure the program is in a common area that is mapped the same on all workstations.

External shortcuts are used to link, among other things, Crystal Reports to the MS Dynamics GP desktop.

XIII.B.6. Add a Folder

If too many shortcuts are added to the Navigation Explorer, the list can become unmanageable. Folders allow similar shortcuts to be grouped together. For example, all manufacturing shortcuts can be placed into one folder named MFG. All month end reports can be placed in a folder named MONTH END.

To create a folder, place the cursor on the Home icon, right click, select Add and then Folder from the configuration menu. A folder with the name New Folder will be created. Right click the folder, select Rename, and enter the appropriate folder name.

Shortcuts can now be dragged into the folder as described below.

XIII.B.7. Organizing the Shortcuts

Items in the Navigation Explorer can be moved easily. Simply select an item and drag and drop to the desired location within the explorer. If folders have been added as described above, shortcuts can be dropped into folders and the list of shortcuts within the folder can be organized.

By right clicking on any shortcut, the Shortcut Properties window is opened. The Name and Keyboard Shortcut assigned to the shortcut can be changed as desired.

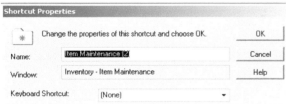

XIII.B.8. Delete Shortcuts

Shortcuts can be deleted by selecting them from the Navigation Explorer, right clicking on the item, and selecting Delete from the menu.

XIII.C. *Modifying the Home Page*

Modifying the Home Page can make MS Dynamics GP much easier to use. Common functions, reminders, important metrics, access to Microsoft Office Outlook can all be placed on the desktop, placing information and power at the user's fingertips.

There are a significant number of changes that can be made to the Home Page. Additionally, almost all of the configuration options have more than one way get to the customization windows.

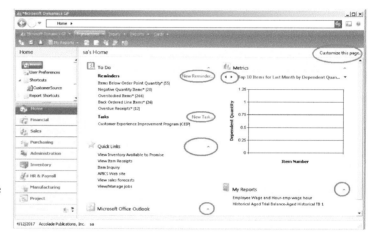

With the Home Page displayed, notice the Customize this page prompt in the upper right corner. Clicking this link will open the Customize Your Home Page window. From that window, other windows used to customize individual sections of the Home Page can be accessed.

Other links scattered throughout the Home Page lead the user to specific customization windows. Now while all of these specific windows can be reached from the main Customize Your Home Page window, users may use these links for quick access to the specific windows.

XIII.C.1. Customizing the Home Page

Clicking the Customize this page prompt in the upper right corner of the Home Page opens the Customize Home Page window.

This window allows several basic selections to be made defining the groups of items that will be displayed on the Home Page and the position of those items.

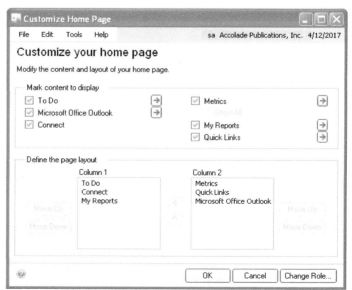

In the top half of the window is the Mark Content to Display group. There are several checkboxes. The user can select to display or not display the associated items by checking or un-checking the boxes. Check the box to the left of each item group to display on the Home Page.

The Expansion Arrows (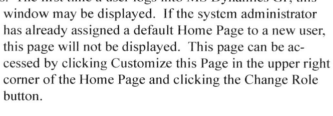) to the right of each item opens configuration windows for the selected window. These windows will be discussed in the pages that follow.

The bottom half of the window is used to define the Home Page layout. Each selected item appears in either the Column 1 or Column 2 window. Each can be selected and an arrow clicked to move the item to the other column. Items can also be highlighted and the Move Up or Move Down buttons used to change its position in the column.

At the bottom of the Customize Home Page window, in addition to the OK and Cancel buttons is found a Change Role Button. Clicking this button re-opens the Select Home Page window.

XIII.C.2. Select the Home Page

Microsoft Dynamics GP ships with a number of predefined Home Page configurations. Many times, simply selecting the correct Home Page configuration is all that is needed to give the user access to frequently used functions. The first time a user logs into MS Dynamics GP, this window may be displayed. If the system administrator has already assigned a default Home Page to a new user, this page will not be displayed. This page can be accessed by clicking Customize this Page in the upper right corner of the Home Page and clicking the Change Role button.

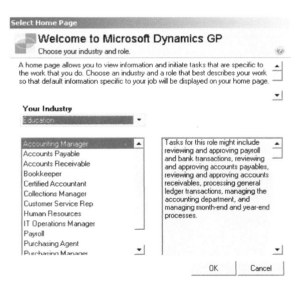

THIS IS NOT A SECURITY ROLE!

Default Home Pages exist for a variety of business functions for 14 different industries. Select in the Industry pull down field an industry that most closely matches the firm's business.

In the scrolling list below the Your Industry field, select the user's role within the firm. This will select a default Home Page with functions close to the user's needs. If a default Home Page cannot be found in the list, the last option is titled Basic Home Page. Select this one!

Keep in mind that selecting a new user role or basic Home Page will wipe out any customization that has already been made to the user's Home Page. Be careful before entering this window.

XIII.C.3. To Do Details

Clicking on the To Do Expansion arrow on the Customize Home Page
window, or highlighting the To Do Title Bar on the Home Page and
then clicking on the pencil icon opens the To Do Details window. Four
different groups of items can be selected by checking the
appropriate boxes on this window.

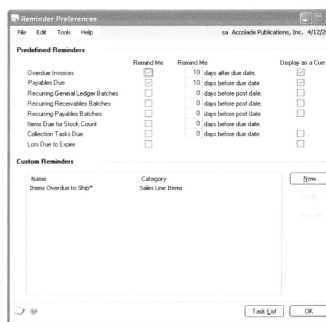

Reminders -- Checking the Reminders box will display
dynamically driven reminders. These items will
appear on the Home Page only when the associated
task needs to be performed.

Tasks -- Checking the Microsoft Dynamics Tasks box
shows a list of predefined tasks the user frequently
performs. These tasks provide a one-click launch
for the items displayed.

Microsoft Workflow Tasks -- Checking this box allows
workflow tasks to be displayed.

Microsoft Workflow Notifications -- Checking this box allows workflow notifications to appear on the Home Page

XIII.C.3.a. Adding or Deleting Reminders

Reminders are added or removed from the desktop using the Reminder
Preferences window. Clicking on the Reminders Expansion arrow on
the To Do Details window, or New Reminders hyper-link on the Home
Page opens the Reminder Preferences window.

Predefined Reminders are listed at the top of the window
and can be added or removed from the desktop by checking or clearing the Remind Me checkbox. The Remind Me
column is used to tailor the reminders to limit the display to
the counts considered critical by the user.

The items can be displayed immediately or a few days
before or after the key dates. For example, to have a count
of Overdue Invoices appear as a line in the reminders and
include only those invoices that are 45 days past due, check
the Overdue Invoices reminder and place 45 in the second
column. The message "Overdue Invoices (99)" will appear
on in the list of Reminders with the number of invoices
older than 45 days old shown.

In Versions 2010 and newer, Reminders can be shown as
text or as a graphical representation. A check box to the
far right allows the user to indicate the type of display. To

show the Reminder as a text line, leave the Display as a Queue box unchecked. To show a graphical representation of the reminder, check the Display as a Queue check box.

Custom reminders are listed in the lower half of the window. These are easily removed by highlighting the reminder and clicking the Remove button. They are added by clicking the New button and opening the Custom Reminder edit window.

Click on the Lookup icon next to the SmartList Favorite field to open and display a list of SmartList favorites. All favorites including custom created and named favorites as well as the default favorites (the ones named *) are available. The name of the reminder will be taken from the name of the SmartList Favorite. Using the favorites named * is not recommended as the only name on the Reminders list on the desktop will be *. Select the SmartList Favorite best suited to provide the information needed to trigger the Reminder.

In the lower portion of the Custom Reminder window, the criteria are defined. There are two options.

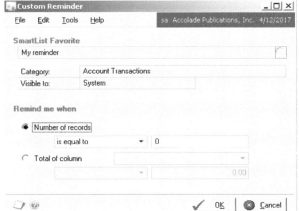

Number of Records -- If this option is marked, then by completing two additional fields, the user specifies that the Reminder should appear when the number of records selected by the SmartList Favorite either is equal to, is greater than, is less than, or is not equal to the value listed in the second field. Select the matching criteria and enter a record count.

Total of Column -- If this option is marked, then one of the columns that appears in the SmartList Favorite is selected. A value is entered into the third field and in the second field matching criteria is selected. Based on the selection, if the field total is equal to, greater than, less than, or is not equal to the value entered in the last field, the reminder will be displayed.

Only one of the above two options can be selected!

When the parameters are set as desired, click the OK button to save the Favorite and the Reminder!

XIII.C.3.b. Adding or Deleting Tasks

Tasks are jobs that are assigned to users. A task can be assigned as a one time event or a recurring job. Any user that has rights to assign tasks can create a task and have that task show up on their own desktop or on another user's desktop. It can be a very handy tool for department managers to assign jobs to others in their team. For example, the

Sales Manager may assign the printing of a series or group of reports to a particular sales administrator. Instead of sending a memo, the Sales Manager can create a task and assign it to the administrative person. A user that has a particular series of periodic tasks to perform each month, each week, or even every 4 days can create a task that will appear on their own desktop to remind them to perform the task.

When a task has been performed, it will clear off the user's desktop. If the task is a one time only task, it is done and over. If the task is a re-curring task, MS Dynamics GP will re-display the task at the scheduled time.

Clicking on the Tasks Expansion arrow on the To Do Details window, or New Tasks hyper-link on the Home Page or the Tasks button on the Reminders Preferences window opens the Task List window. The Task List window lists all tasks, the user the task is assigned to, the due date of the task, the date the task is completed, and the ID of the user that completed the task.

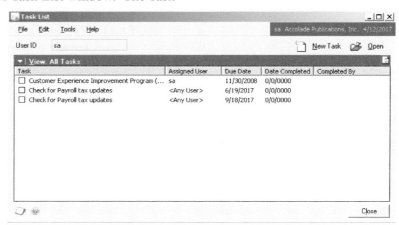

The View menu pull down (left edge of the column headers) allows the user to limit the list of tasks to All Tasks, Completed Tasks only, or Pending Tasks only.

To Add a New Task . . .

Click on the New Task icon on the Task List window. The Task window will open. Complete the fields as desired.

Task -- Enter a short description of the task. This information will be displayed in the task descriptions.

Due Date -- Enter the next due date for this task. If the task will be a recurring task, enter the first due date. The task will be displayed on the Home Page on this date and will remain on the Home Page until it has been completed.

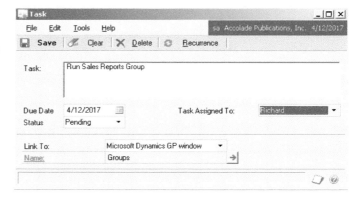

Status -- Initially, this should be set to Pending. Once the task has been completed, it will be changed to Completed.

Task Assigned To -- Select from the pull down list, the user that should perform this task. There is also a special selection called <any user> which will place the task on every user's desktop and it will remain there until one person completes the task. It would be nice if the tasks could be assigned to Classes of users but that is not supported yet (contact Microsoft!!) The ID of the user creating the task will be defaulted into this field.

Link To -- This pull down menu starts the process of linking the task to a specific task in MS Dynamics GP. Open the pull down menu and select the appropriate source of the task link.

> **No Link** -- The task will be displayed, but it will not be linked to any specific task.

> **Microsoft Dynamics GP Window** -- The task will be linked to a MS Dynamics GP task.

> **Web Page** -- The task will be linked to a Web Page

> **External Program or File** -- The task will be linked to an external program, like Excel or Crystal Reports.

Name -- This field specifies the task to be executed to complete the task. The information entered here depends on the value selected in the Link To field above:

> **No Link** -- The field is not active.

> **Microsoft Dynamics GP Window** -- Clicking on the expansion arrow on the right end of the field will open an explorer. The user can browse down the explorer to locate the MS Dynamics GP task desired.

> **Web Page** -- The user must enter a URL of a web page.

> **External Program** -- A Browse button allows the user to browse programs on the network and select the task to be executed.

When the information has been entered as desired, click the Save button to record the task. If the task is to be a Recurring task, set the schedule as described below before saving the task.

To Make the Task Recurring . . .

While defining a task using the Task window, click on the Recurrence button on the Task window's tool bar. The Recurrence window will open.

Set the Recurrence Pattern. Options include Daily, Weekly, Monthly, Yearly, Every number of days, or Every Weekday. Only one option can be selected. If the user specifies Every number of days, then the number of days between recurrences must be specified. The difference between Daily and Every Weekday are weekends. The task will not be scheduled to occur on Saturday and Sunday if Every Weekday is selected.

Specify the Range of Recurrences... A Start date needs to be specified. It will default to the Due Date on the Task window. Ranges include:

> **No End Date** -- The task will recur at the frequency specified until the task is manually edited.

> **End After** -- A number of occurrences is specified. After the task has been performed that number of times, the system will no longer reschedule it.

> **End By** -- An end date for the task is specified. The task will be rescheduled until the end date is reached.

When the recurrences have been defined as desired, click the OK button to return to the Task window. On the Task window, click the Save button to save the task.

To manually delete a reoccurrence schedule, open the task, click on the Recurrence button, and click on the Remove Recurrence button. Save the edited task.

To Modify an Existing Task . . .

From the Task List window, highlight a task and click the Open button. The Task window will open. Any of the information can be edited, including recurrences, and the changed task saved.

To Delete a Task . . .

From the Task List window, highlight a task and click the Open button. The Task window will open. Click on the Delete button on the Task window.

XIII.C.4.   Changing the Quick Links

Quick Links are shortcuts that appear on the Home Page. Just like Tasks, they link the user to frequently performed tasks. Unlike Tasks, Quick Links are not tied to any schedule and remain on the Home Page just like a shortcut remains in the Navigation Explorer.

Quick Links are helpful in reducing key strokes to get to frequently performed tasks. For example, if the user is always using the Sales Transaction Entry window, they can click on Transactions → Sales → Transaction Entry. However, if a Quick Link is built, the user can simply click on the Sales Transaction Entry Quick Link and the window opens immediately.

To edit the Quick Links, place the cursor in the Quick Links title bar on the Home Page and click on the pencil icon. The Quick Links Details window will open.

To change the order of the Quick Links . . .

Highlight a Quick Link and use the Move Up or Move Down button to move the link to the desired place in the list.

To Delete a Quick Link .. .

Highlight the Quick Link to delete and click on the Delete button.

To Modify an Existing Quick Link . . .

Highlight the Quick Link to be edited and click on the Modify button. The appropriate window (based on the type of link) will open. The information can be changed as needed and saved. See To Add a Quick Link below for information on each type of link.

To Add a New Quick Link . . .

Click on the Add button and a pull down menu will appear. There are 4 types of Quick Links that can be created:

Microsoft Dynamics GP Window -- Select this option and the Add Command window opens displaying the Tool Bar menu options. The user can select from Transactions, Inquiry, Reports, Cards, et cetera. Once the type of transaction is selected, the pull down menu tree will be displayed in an Explorer format. Locate the desired task and click OK.

Microsoft Dynamics GP Navigation List --Select this option and an Add List window will open displaying the List Views available in the Navigation Pane. Drill down in the Explorer display of the Navigation Explorer, locate the desired List View, highlight it and click OK.

Web Page -- Select this option and the Add Web Page window will be displayed. Enter a Name to be displayed in the Quick Links on the Home Page and the URL of the desired web page. Click OK to save the new Quick Link.

External Program or File -- Selecting this option opens the Add External Program window. Enter a Name for the Quick Link to appear on the Home Page. Then use the Browse button to locate the appropriate program to be run. Click OK to save the new Quick Link.

XIII.C.5. Changing the Metrics

Metrics are those charts and graphs that display on the Home Page. They can be disabled by clicking the Customize this Page hyper-link or from the Customize Home Page window un-check the Metrics option. The metrics will not be displayed.

If metrics are being displayed, the user can select from a number of predefined charts. In Chapter III.E.1.e, the on-screen metrics are discussed and instructions are found that allow the user to select from a short list of charts. However, the shortlist is also configurable!

To edit the list of charts that can be displayed, either click on the Customize this Page link on the Home Page and then click on the Expansion Arrow next to the Metrics listing, or click on the Metrics label on the Home Page and then click on the pencil. The Metrics Details window will be displayed.

The Metrics Details window consists of two panes: the Metrics Available and the Metrics to Display list. In the Metrics Available list are all of the charts that could be viewed through the MS Dynamics GP Home Page. In the Metrics to Display list are all of the charts currently available from the Home page.

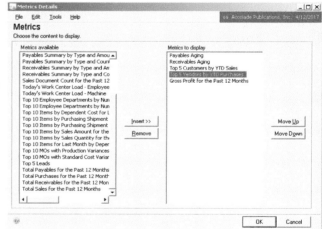

For a user to be able to view a particular chart on the Home Page, the chart must appear in the Metrics to Display list.

To add a chart to the Metrics to Display list . ..

Highlight the desired chart in the left pane and click the Insert button.

To Remove a Chart from the Metrics to Display list . . .

Highlight a chart in the right pane and click the Remove button.

To Change the Sequence of the Charts . . .

Highlight a chart in the right pane and use the Move Up or Move Down button to move the chart in the list.

When all of the changes to the metrics have been completed, click the OK button.

XIII.C.6. Changing the My Reports List

The My Reports list displays a group of Report Options that are selected frequently by a user. By placing the Report Option on the My Reports list, the user can select the report quickly from one location. There are a couple of ways to place a report on the My Reports list.

When a report is executed on the Reports Menu, a Report Option needs to be defined. During the definition of the Report Option, the user can add the report to their My Reports list. See Chapter VI.A. for information on creating a report option and adding the option to the My Reports list.

Each module or series has a Reports List leaf in the Navigation Explorer. Select the desired series by clicking on the appropriate tile in the Navigation Pane (Sales, Purchasing, Financial, et cetera). Then in the Navigation Explorer, browse down near the bottom of the list and click on the Reports List leaf. The Reports List View will be displayed in the Content Pane.

Select a report from the List View. Select only one report at a time. If multiple reports are selected, the Add To option will not be active. With one report selected (click the check box to the left of the report), the Add To button in the My Reports section of the Action Pane is active. Click the Add To button.

An Add to My Reports window will now appear. The current Name of the report will be displayed. Change the name if desired and click the OK button. The report will be added to the My Reports list on the Home Page.

To remove a report from the My Reports list, click on the My Reports title bar on the Home Page, then click on the Pencil icon to open the My Reports List view. Select the report to be removed by clicking the check box to the left of the report. Then click the Remove From icon in the My Reports section of the Action Pane.

XIII.D. Creating List Views

MS Dynamics GP is delivered with a group of standard lists as well as a number of customized versions of these lists. Users can create their own customized lists from the existing lists. The process involves entering filters to specify a subset of the records displayed and then saving the specifications under a new name. These new lists are called List Views.

Select a list that contains the information desired. This list is then shortened to a more concise list by applying a series of filters. Filters can be logical : And, Or, Not, or Either statements. Fields are matched to user provided data and can be required to exactly match, begin with, contain, be greater than, less than, or not equal to the user data. Fields that are empty can also be selected.

Fairly complex conditional statements can be constructed using combinations of the comparison types and logical operators.

Each piece of the filter is added by clicking on the Add Filter prompt. The Logical Operator type is selected from a pull down list. The field to be used in the comparison is then selected from a pull down list. Next, the comparison type is selected, and finally the data to be used to limit the list is entered. Additional statements can be added by clicking on the Add Filter prompt until the logical statement is complete and the desired data is shown in the list.

Once the desired filter is built, it can be saved. The user clicks on the pull down arrow (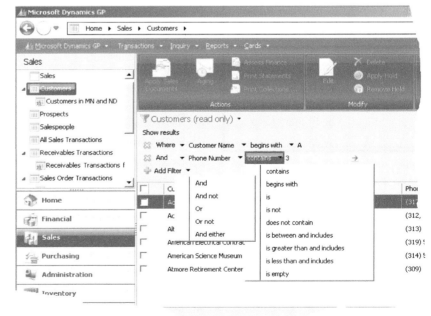) next to the title line of the original list. Select the Save As option on the pull down menu and enter a name for the new list. The new list will be listed as a variation of the original list. It will be found in the Navigation Pane Explorer by expanding the primary list from which it was created. For example, if a Customer list is modified to show only customers in a specified state and is saved, the new list option will be displayed in the Navigation Pane Explorer when the expansion arrow next to Customers is clicked.

If the user clicks Add to the Navigation Pane as a Shortcut, the name of the new list is added to the Home Navigation Explorer. It can be seen in the Navigation

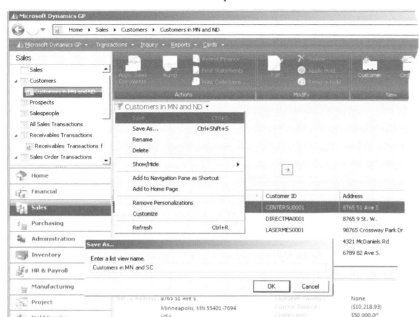

Explorer when the Home Tile is clicked and the Home Page displayed in the Content Pane. Clicking on the entry will open the new list in the Content Pane immediately.

If the user clicks Add to the Home Page, the name of the new list will be added to the Home Page itself and displayed in the Content Pane under Quick Links. The new list can then be displayed by clicking on the Quick Link.

To delete a List View, select the list from the Navigation Pane Explorer, click on the pull down arrow next to the list name in the Content Pane, and select Delete.

A list can be renamed by selecting the list from the Navigation Pane Explorer, clicking on the pull down arrow next to the list name in the Content Pane, and selecting Rename.

XIII.D.1. Customizing the Content of a List

Only List Views Can Be Modified!

Only a List View, a customization created from a Primary List, can be modified. The Primary Lists cannot be modified.

The content of customized lists or List Views, including the columns of data displayed and the contents of the Action Pane can be modified to suit the needs of the user. The new list can be held as a private list available only to the user that created the list or shared among other users and other companies.

With the desired List View displayed, click on the down arrow next to the list name to open the List Options menu. Select Customize. The List View Customization window is displayed. (The Customize option will ONLY be available for List Views and NOT for Primary Lists.)

If the MS Dynamics GP implementation supports multiple companies, the user can select the company in which the list will be displayed, or optionally, have the list available in all companies. In the Content to Display box, the user can indicate whether Filter Options, the Action Pane, and the Information Pane should be displayed by default when the list first opens.

The real power to customizing a list is found in the Modify List View section of the window. Here, the data is displayed, along with contents of the Action Pane, and sharing of the list with other users is defined.

XIII.D.2. Selecting Columns to Display

By clicking on the Columns expansion button on the List View Customization window, the Column
Details window is opened. This
window lists the available data
columns that can be displayed in
the list.

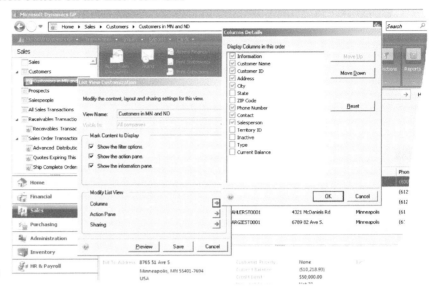

Columns are added or removed
from the list display by checking or un-checking boxes next
to the column names in the list.
The order of the columns can be
changed by highlighting a column
name and clicking the Move Up or
Move Down button.

When the column list is marked
and sequenced as desired, click the
OK button to close the window.

XIII.D.3. Selecting Actions for the List

The contents of the Action Pane can be modified for the List View.
With the List View Customization window displayed, click on the Action Pane Expansion Arrow. The Action Pane Details window will be
displayed.

Each of the groups found in the Action Pane of the Primary List are
found in the Groups List in the window. New groups can be added,
existing groups removed, the name of the group can be edited, and the
order of the groups rearranged.

To add a Group, click on the Add Group button. The Groups window
will be displayed listing all available Groups that can be added to the
Action Pane. The list of valid Groups is found in the side-bar note and
includes two User Defined Groups. Select the desired Group and click
the Select button to add the Group to the Groups List in the Action
Pane Details window.

To remove a Group, highlight the Group in the Groups list and click
on the Remove Group button. Only click once or more than one group
will be removed. To change the sequence of the Groups in the Action
Pane, click on a Group in the Groups List and use the Up and Down
buttons to move the Group in the list.

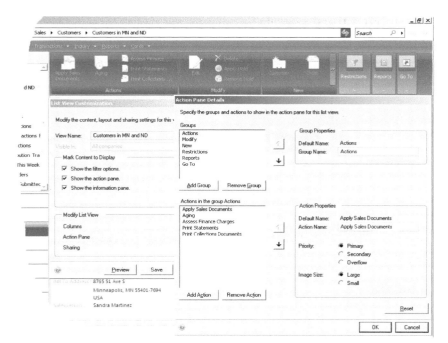

A Group Name can be changed in the Group Properties area of the Action Pane Details window. Click on the desired group in the Groups List and that Group's properties will be displayed in the Group Properties area. The Default Name cannot be changed and is the name the system uses to identify the Group. The Group Name, however, can be changed. It is the Group Name that is displayed in the Action Pane.

Actions in each Group are defined in the lower half of the Action Pane Details window. Actions can be added or removed from any Group, the sequence of the action in the pane can be changed, the priority of the action (in the event the window is resized) changed, and the display name modified if necessary.

Select the Group to be modified by clicking on it in the Group list in the top half of the window. The list of actions for that Group will be displayed in the Actions In the Group list.

To add an Action to the Group, click on the Add Action Button. The Actions window seen below will be displayed, listing all of the available Actions that can be added to a Group. Select the desired Action and click the Select button to add it to the Group. (The list of actions is different for each Series). It is the user's responsibility to make sure the correct type of action is added to the correct group. For example, the Edit action (which opens the selected record's edit window, such as the Customer Maintenance window for the Customer List) can be added to the Reports Group, an obvious error.

To remove an Action from the Group, click on the Action and click the Remove Action Button. To change the sequence of Actions within the Group, click on the Action and click the Up or Down Arrow button to move the Action up or down in the list.

There are several properties that can be set for an Action in the Action Properties area. The Default Name of the Action cannot be changed. It is the name the system uses to refer to the Action. The Action Name is the title displayed in the Action Pane and can be changed as desired. For example, the Edit Action might be renamed Edit Customer.

The Priority setting determines how the Action is treated if re-sizing of the window makes it impossible for all of the Actions to be displayed in the Group. As the area available on the desktop is reduced, Actions are removed from the desktop and placed in the overflow pull down list. Actions marked with the priority Overflow will always appear in the Overflow pull down. Actions marked with a priority of Secondary will be moved into the Overflow first. Only when all Secondary Actions are in the Overflow pull down will Actions marked Primary be moved into the pull down.

The Image Size Property defines the size of the icon displayed for the Action. Only Actions with a priority of Primary or Secondary will have this property available as only one size icon is shown in the Overflow menu. However, Primary and Secondary priority Actions can be displayed with either a Large or Small icon. Important tasks should have large icons. Marking tasks to be displayed with small icons will allow more tasks to be displayed in the Action Pane.

Make sure to save the changes made to the Action Pane by clicking the OK button to close the Action Pane Details window, and then the Save button on the List View Customization.

Action Pane Groups

The following are valid Groups that can be displayed in the Action Pane. These Groups are selected in the Action Pane Details window and can be renamed by the user.

Action
Modify
New
Restrictions
Reports
GoTo
User Defined Group 1
User Defined Group 2

A wide variety of Actions is available to be added to any group.

XIII.D.4. Sharing Lists with Others

List Views can be held private and viewed only by the user that created the view, or made available to other users in the company. This is controlled by using the Sharing Expansion Arrow on the List View Customization window. The Sharing Details window will be displayed.

Two radio buttons at the top of the window provide the first level of control. If the list is only to be viewed by the user that creates the list, then that user should check the Private radio button. To make the list public, the Public radio button must be checked. Once the Public button is checked, specific users and or Roles can be added to the access list.

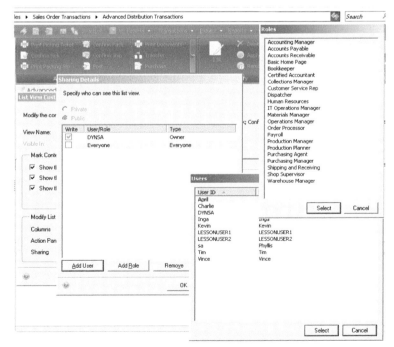

Users are given access to the list by clicking the Add User button on the Sharing Details Window. The Users list will be displayed. Users can be selected and added to the List View by clicking the Select Button.

Groups of users can be given access to a List View by adding Roles to the Sharing Details window. Click on the Add Role button and the list of defined business Roles will be displayed. Highlight the desired Roles and click the Select button. The Role, and all users that are members of that Role will be given access to the List View. Only the Role will be displayed in the Sharing Details window. To control individual user's access, use Add Users rather than Add Roles.

Users and Roles added to the Sharing Details list will only have View rights to the List View. While they may be able to edit the data displayed in the List view through selected Actions, they cannot change the structure of the List View. To give the users or Roles (and their members) rights to modify the list data, check the Write box next to the user(s) or Role(s) that should have permission to make changes. Users and Roles that have Write permissions can make changes to the List View.

To remove a user or Role (group of users) from a List View, select the user or Role and click the Remove button. To save changes to the access rights, click the OK button on the Sharing Details window and then click Save on the List View Customization window.

XIII.D.5. Security and the Action Pane

The MS Dynamics GP role based security system determines which users have access to which functions. This includes access to lists and the ability to execute the functions found in the Action Pane. If an Action is included in the Action Pane for a List and a user has rights to view the list that contains that Action but does not have the rights to the Action itself, the Action will not appear in the Action Pane for that user.

For example, suppose Patty has access to the Customer List but does not have rights to add or modify customer records. The Edit Records action is included in the Customer List. When Patty displays the Customer List, the Edit Action will not be displayed since Patty has no authority to perform that function.

XIII.E. Setting User Preferences

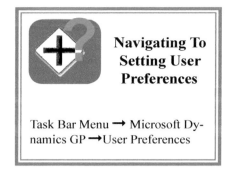

Navigating To Setting User Preferences

Task Bar Menu → Microsoft Dynamics GP →User Preferences

The User Preferences window allows individual users to set personal preferences to customize their installation of MS Dynamics GP. The preferences set in this screen are recorded for the user logged into the workstation and will follow the user to any other workstation when they use their user id and password to sign in to MS Dynamics GP.

The User Preferences screen is located under Microsoft Dynamics GP → User Preferences. Many sites disable this screen when setting security since most of the other functions on the Microsoft Dynamics GP menu should be locked down. If access to this window is blocked, encourage the System Administrator to relax the rules just a bit and turn on access to the User Preferences window.

The User Preferences window allows individual users to set the following preferences:

Horizontal Scroll Arrows -- This check box enables horizontal scroll arrows to be displayed next to account number fields if the firm's account number is longer than the display window. Most display windows will show 12 to 15 digits of an account number, plenty for most firms. However, since MS Dynamics GP allows account numbers as long as 66 characters, in some cases these 12-15 character windows are too small.

Default Report Destination -- When a report allows a user to specify its destination, the default destination is taken from this set of option buttons. Check Printer to have the Printer box defaulted and Screen to have the Screen box checked on the Report Destination window.

Entry Key -- This set of options allows a user to use the Enter key to advance to the next field rather than the Tab key. The Windows standard, as well as the main frame standard for data entry is that Tab keys move the focus (the active field) from the current field to the next field in the window. DOS applications used the Enter key. Users switching from DOS applications to Windows applications sometimes find it difficult to remember to hit the Tab key. This option allows users to change the default action to the Enter key. It is recommended that this switch of functions NOT be selected as the current standard for ALL Windows tasks is to use the Tab key to move from field to field.

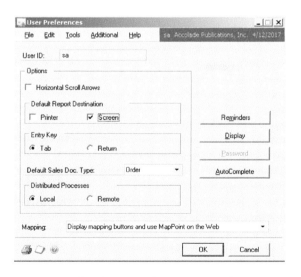

Default Sales Document Type -- If the firm is using Sales Order Processing, this determines the default document type when the Sales Transaction Entry window is first opened. For customer service team members, it is important to set this field to the most frequently used document type. Options include Quote, Order, Fulfillment Order, Invoice, Return, and Back Order.

Distributed Processes -- MS Dynamics GP allows certain processes that normally run in the background on the local workstation to be off-loaded to a Process Server. Before this option can be used, a Process Server must be setup, and configured. The normal setting for this option is Local, indicating that the background tasks will run on the local machine. If a Process Server is available, the Remote option will allow certain tasks to be off loaded to that machine.

Mapping -- The Map Pins scattered throughout the application and attached to address fields allow the display of a map. These maps automatically display the address in the adjacent fields. This option allows a user to disable the display of the MapPoint buttons or select the source of the maps. A local copy of MapPoint or an Internet connection can be used to obtain mapping data.

XIII.E.1. Display Button

The user's display attributes can be modified by making the following selections in the User Display Preferences window. This window is opened when the user clicks the Display button on the User Preferences window.

The User Display Preferences window has two sections. Options are selected in the lower half of the window. When the Apply button is clicked, the selected changes are shown in the upper half of the window.

Scheme -- Three different color schemes are supported by MS Dynamics GP. The user can select any of the three schemes.

Underline Prompts -- Checking this box extends a small line from the bottom of the data entry field through the bottom of the prompt. Turn this option on and off by clicking the Apply button to see the effects.

Link Fields -- Link fields are those fields that, when the prompt is clicked, open other windows. The Font Color and Style can be changed for link fields. The default is Blue and Underline.

Required Fields -- Required fields are those fields that must be completed before a screen can be processed. To make these fields stand out on all screens, set the Required Fields color and font style. We recommend Red and Bold. To enable these changes, the Show Required Fields option under Help in the top tool bar of Dynamics GP must be checked.

XIII.E.2. Password Button

The Password Button allows a user to change their own MS Dynamics GP password. The user is required to enter their old password as well as the new password to make the change.

XIII.E.3. Auto Complete Button

The following options are set by clicking the Auto Complete button on the User Preferences screen.

Show Auto Complete Suggestions -- With this box checked, the system will remember the last entries made into each field and offer them as selectable options. Un-checking this box disables the Auto Complete function.

Remove Unused Entries After -- The number in this field specifies the number of days to retain entries in the Auto-Complete list. If too many entries are retained, windows may take a long time to load. The default entry is zero (0) which keeps Auto Complete entries forever. We recommend setting this field to 20 days or less.

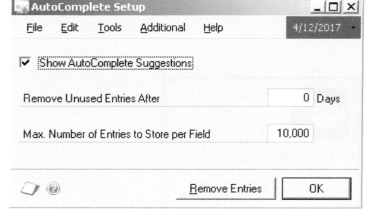

Maximum Number of Entries to Store per Field -- As it suggests, the number in this field is the maximum number of Auto Complete entries the system will store per field. The default is 10,000. If a window has 20 or more fields and must load up to 10,000 options for each field, the time to load the window can be long. It is strongly recommended that this number be reduced to 100-300.

Remove Entries -- Clicking this button will erase all Auto Complete entries stored for the current user.

XIII.E.4. Reminders

Yes, the reminders for a user can also be set from this window. See Chapter XIII.C.3.a. for information on using the Reminders Preferences window.

The Dynamics GP Power User Guidebook

Change Your Password

Users can change their own Dynamics GP password.

Under Microsoft Dynamics → User Preferences → Password, enter the logged on user's original password and then enter the desired new password. The new password must be entered twice to confirm that it was properly entered.

XIII.F. System Preferences Window

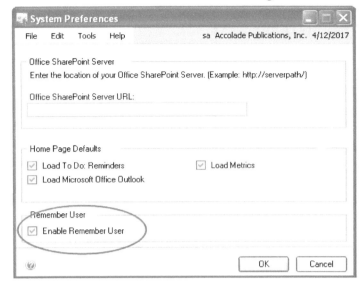

Starting with Version 2010, the System Preferences window has been enhanced to support the configuration of the Remember the User feature of the Login window.

At the bottom of the System Preferences window is a check box that enables the Remember User function on the Login window. Check the box to enable users to login without entering their User ID and password. The system will use the User ID and password of the last user to have logged on at the workstation.

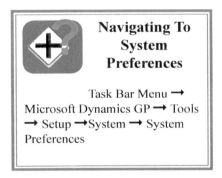

Navigating To System Preferences

Task Bar Menu → Microsoft Dynamics GP → Tools → Setup →System → System Preferences

XIV.   Dynamics GP Macros

MS Dynamics GP has a Macro Language built in. Some users may be familiar with the ability to record and playback macro scripts. Few know of the full power of the language and the commands that can be added to a script but not recorded. In these pages we will discuss the basics of recording and playing back macros. Details on the Macro Language can be found in *Confessions of a Dynamics GP Consultant I*.

Navigating To Macros

Task Bar Menu → Microsoft Dynamics GP → Tools → Macro

Microsoft uses the macro language to test the application during development. Prior to the existence of import and export features in the report writer and windows modifier, consultants used the macro facility to record changes to reports and windows and move those changes to other user's systems.

XIV.A.   Macro Basics

Using the macro menu options, users can record a series of keystrokes and repeatedly playback that recorded sequence. For example, adding new inventory items frequently requires a user to enter the same pricing structure over and over again for each new item as well as create Quantity/Site records and set Item Purchasing Options. If all of these fields are set exactly the same for a group of items, a user can enter the unique data on the Item Card, click ALT+F8 key to start recording a macro, enter the data on the Price List, Quantity/Site, and Purchasing Options, return to the Item Card to begin the entry of the next item, and click Alt/F8 again to stop the recording. Then, after entering the unique data for the next item on the Item Card, the user can click Ctrl/F8, pick the saved macro, and the system will automatically replay the keystrokes and build the Price List, Quantity/Site, and Purchasing Options screens. This ability saves countless keystrokes and ensures that all sites are setup the same, all price list entries are the same (assuming a percentage of list or cost price method is in use), et cetera.

When a macro is created, (by the user hitting the Alt/F8 key combination) a text file is created. The user must name the text file and specify the place where it will be stored. As the user then performs the original set of steps in record mode, Dynamics GP adds lines to this text file. During playback mode, Dynamics GP reads the text file and executes the recorded commands.

Macro text files do not need to be stored on the local PC and can be shared on a public drive. A macro recorded by one user can be played back by other users provided that both users (or all users that might use the macro) have the same screens. If any modified screens are installed, those modified screens must exist on all workstations and all users must have access to them. Otherwise, the macros might fail during playback when it encounters differences in the windows.

XIV.B. Pauses and User Entered Fields

Using the macro menu, pauses can be inserted in a macro. There may be cases when almost every keystroke of a repetitive task is identical except for the data in one or two fields. During the recording of the macro, when the user reaches one of these fields, use the macro menu to Insert a Pause. MS Dynamics GP will stop recording and ask for a prompt or message to be displayed to the user during playback. Specify a message, enter the desired data then, again using the macro menu, resume and complete the recording.

Now, during the playback of this macro, the system will playback to the point where the pause was inserted and display the recorded prompt in a message box. Click OK to close the message box, enter the desired data in the field or fields, then resume playback. Playback can be resumed by using the macro menu. The keyboard shortcut to resume playback is Alt/T/M/C (hold the Alt key then hit T, M, then C).

XIV.C. Silencing the Macro

When a macro runs to completion, it displays a message "Macro xxxxx Ran for 4.3 Seconds". Most people do not care about this message and find the extra keystroke to close the window bothersome. The macro can be edited to eliminate the message.

After the macro has been recorded, edit the text file in Notepad or any text editor (don't use Word!). Insert the following line at the top of the macro file:

> LOGGING file *'x:/path/filename.txt'*

Change *x:/path/filename.txt* to the name of a text file in a common shared folder.

With this command inserted, when the macro runs, the messages will be written to the logging text file named in the command and not shown on screen.

XIV.D. Macros and Shortcuts

Macros, once recorded, can be listed on the Navigation Pane as a shortcut. Open the Navigation Pane, click on the Add icon, and select Macro from the menu. Enter a display name for the macro and enter the name of the macro file in the Macro File field (or browse to it). Click Add to add the shortcut to the Navigation Pane. The macro can now be run by double clicking on the new shortcut on the Navigation Pane.

While adding the shortcut, a Keyboard Shortcut can be selected. If one is specified (select an available shortcut key from the pull down list) the macro can then be run simply by clicking the selected key combination.

XIV.E.   *Mail Merge Macro*

The entry of a large amount of data into MS Dynamics GP (or any application) can be a time consuming activity. Some firms invest in the Integration Manager and use that tool to import data. In some cases, Integration Manger does not provide a destination adapter and the user may not be trained in the direct to table adapter or unsure about all of the business logic that occurs during the entry of the data or the tables that are updated.

Using the macro system to record the data entry process and then expanding it to repeat for each item to be loaded is another way to import data. We call this the Mail Merge Macro since the Word mail merge function is used to expand the macro. Here is how it works.

Lets use, as an example, a firm that needs to setup identical manufacturing routers for 150 new products. Through Integration Manager, the items have been imported. The Integration Manager, however, does not provide an import for router information. Here are the steps to create a macro to perform this task.

1.   Record a macro and enter the router for the first two items. It is easier to identify the repeating steps if two or more passes through the process have been recorded. Stop the recording.

2   Open the macro file that was recorded in Word. Identify the repeating lines of the macro and save these to another document. Save the document as a text document.

3.   Open the new document and turn it into a Word Mail Merge document. Insert mail-merge fields into the macro code where item numbers or other changing data needs to be inserted.

4.   Use SmartList or some other tool to export the list of item numbers and any other fields that need to be inserted into the mail merged document. Save it as a CSV file.

5.   Merge the two files, creating a long macro with a repeating section for each item in the CSV file.

6.   Replace any lines removed from the beginning or end of the macro. (Note: if the original macro was recorded properly, starting exactly where the repeating steps begin and ending at exactly that same spot, there will be no missing lines.)

7.   Edit the merged document one more time to replace some spe-

cial codes that Word will insert. Use the Replace function and open the More → Special tab and select Section Breaks to be replaced. Replace them with the Paragraph Marks also found under Special.

8. Save the merged document as a text file. This gets rid of the paragraph marks.

9. Run the macro. The new items will be setup.

Index

Subscribe to our
FREE Newsletter

It's Filled with Helpful Hints and News on
Dynamics GP
and
Published Electronically Every Two Weeks

from

Accolade Publications, Inc.

Visit www.AccoladePublications.com
to Subscribe

Start Getting the Help You Need Today!